Home Mortgage Delinquency and Foreclosure

NATIONAL BUREAU OF ECONOMIC RESEARCH

NUMBER 91, GENERAL SERIES

Home Mortgage Delinquency and Foreclosure

John P. Herzog
Simon Fraser University

and

James S. Earley
University of California, Riverside

NATIONAL BUREAU OF ECONOMIC RESEARCH

NEW YORK 1970

Distributed by COLUMBIA UNIVERSITY PRESS

NEW YORK AND LONDON

RELATION OF THE DIRECTORS TO THE
WORK AND PUBLICATIONS OF THE
NATIONAL BUREAU OF ECONOMIC RESEARCH

1. The object of the National Bureau of Economic Research is to ascertain and to present to the public important economic facts and their interpretation in a scientific and impartial manner. The Board of Directors is charged with the responsibility of ensuring that the work of the National Bureau is carried on in strict conformity with this object.

2. The President of the National Bureau shall submit to the Board of Directors, or to its Executive Committee, for their formal adoption all specific proposals for research to be instituted.

3. No research report shall be published until the President shall have submitted to each member of the Board the manuscript proposed for publication, and such information as will, in his opinion and in the opinion of the author, serve to determine the suitability of the report for publication in accordance with the principles of the National Bureau. Each manuscript shall contain a summary drawing attention to the nature and treatment of the problem studied, the character of the data and their utilization in the report, and the main conclusions reached.

4. For each manuscript so submitted, a special committee of the Board shall be appointed by majority agreement of the President and Vice Presidents (or by the Executive Committee in case of inability to decide on the part of the President and Vice Presidents), consisting of three directors selected as nearly as may be one from each general division of the Board. The names of the special manuscript committee shall be stated to each Director when the manuscript is submitted to him. It shall be the duty of each member of the special manuscript committee to read the manuscript. If each member of the manuscript committee signifies his approval within thirty days of the transmittal of the manuscript, the report may be published. If at the end of that period any member of the manuscript committee withholds his approval, the President shall then notify each member of the Board, requesting approval or disapproval of publication, and thirty days additional shall be granted for this purpose. The manuscript shall then not be published unless at least a majority of the entire Board who shall have voted on the proposal within the time fixed for the receipt of votes shall have approved.

5. No manuscript may be published, though approved by each member of the special manuscript committee, until forty-five days have elapsed from the transmittal of the report in manuscript form. The interval is allowed for the receipt of any memorandum of dissent or reservation, together with a brief statement of his reasons, that any member may wish to express; and such memorandum of dissent or reservation shall be published with the manuscript if he so desires. Publication does not, however, imply that each member of the Board has read the manuscript, or that either members of the Board in general or the special committee have passed on its validity in every detail.

6. Publications of the National Bureau issued for informational purposes concerning the work of the Bureau and its staff, or issued to inform the public of activities of Bureau staff, and volumes issued as a result of various conferences involving the National Bureau shall contain a specific disclaimer noting that such publication has not passed through the normal review procedures required in this resolution. The Executive Committee of the Board is charged with review of all such publications from time to time to ensure that they do not take on the character of formal research reports of the National Bureau, requiring formal Board approval.

7. Unless otherwise determined by the Board or exempted by the terms of paragraph 6, a copy of this resolution shall be printed in each National Bureau publication.

(Resolution adopted October 25, 1926 and revised February 6, 1933, February 24, 1941, and April 20, 1968)

CONTENTS

CHARTS

TABLES

Foreword

This monograph is a part of the National Bureau's Quality of Credit Program, which in recent years has studied the changing characteristics and performance of credit in every major sector of the U.S. economy.[1] The enormous postwar growth of one- to four-family home mortgage debt, and the veritable revolution in terms, give special importance to this study.

The study was made possible by the generous assistance of the three leading associations of U.S. mortgage lenders: the U.S. Savings and Loan League, the Mortgage Bankers Association of America, and the National Association of Mutual Savings Banks. They supplied not only financial support but the even more vital sample data. Leon Kendall, Oliver Jones and Saul Klaman represented the three cooperating associations on the project and supervised the three surveys that secured the data.

Other funds for the project were provided by the Research Committee of the Graduate School of the University of Wisconsin and the general funds of the National Bureau. Additional computer time was supplied by Western Data Processing Center at UCLA. The University of Wisconsin's Social Systems Research Institute assisted in analytical design and performed most of the programming. Special thanks are due to

[1] Previously published studies are: Albert M. Wojnilower, *The Quality of Bank Loans: A Study of Bank Examination Records* (1962); Martin H. Seiden, *The Quality of Trade Credit* (1964); Thomas R. Atkinson, assisted by Elizabeth T. Simpson, *Trends in Corporate Bond Quality* (1967); Geoffrey H. Moore and Philip A. Klein, *The Quality of Consumer Instalment Credit* (1967). Several earlier investigations by the National Bureau, published in its Studies in Urban Mortgage Financing, dealt with characteristics of urban mortgages and factors affecting lending experience in the 1920's, 1930's and 1940's. For a summary report, see J. E. Morton, *Urban Mortgage Lending: Comparative Markets and Experience*, Princeton University Press for NBER, 1956.

Donald Steward and Edward Glaaser in this connection. On behalf of the National Bureau I am privileged to thank all of these organizations and persons for their assistance.

We are grateful also to Edgar R. Fiedler, Jack M. Guttentag, and F. Thomas Juster, who served as the staff reading committee of the Bureau; to Robert M. Fisher, Board of Governors of the Federal Reserve System, who supplied useful comments on the report; to Wallace J. Campbell, M. G. de Chazeau, and Walter E. Hoadley of the Director's reading committee; to James F. McRee, Jr., who edited the manuscript, and to H. Irving Forman, who drew the charts.

My colleague, John Herzog, performed the prodigious labor required to convert the raw sample data into material suitable for computer analysis, and drafted all but the first chapter of the monograph and the Introduction and Summary. I gathered the material for the first chapter in preparing my forthcoming volume, *The Quality of Postwar Credit in the United States,* which will summarize the major results of this and other special studies of postwar credit quality. Both Herzog and I are responsible for the design of the study and share responsibility for the interpretation of the results.

James S. Earley
Director, Quality of Credit Program

Introduction and Summary

The growing importance of home mortgage loans in the portfolios of American financial institutions, the radical shift that occurred in the characteristics of these loans over the postwar years, and the considerable rise (albeit from very low levels) in mortgage delinquency and foreclosure in the late 1950's and early 1960's, motivated this study. It examines the characteristics significantly associated with mortgage performance and attempts to measure changes in the quality of home mortgage loans that may have occurred over the postwar years as a result of the changed characteristics.

Chapter I examines changes in home mortgage characteristics and performance in the postwar period, and briefly summarizes other postwar studies of characteristics as related to performance. Chapter II, which is the heart of the investigation, applies multiple regression analyses to nationwide sample data covering nearly 13,000 home mortgage loans to ascertain how various characteristics were related to the performance status of the loans in the year 1963. Chapter III uses these relationships, combined with time series data on characteristics, to measure changes in home mortgage quality through time.

There have been marked changes in home mortgage loan and borrower characteristics over the postwar years. In the latter 1950's and early 1960's an increasing share of borrowing was for refinancing purposes, as distinct from the purchase of a new property. There is also evidence of a growth of junior financing accompanying home mortgage borrowing over these years. Typical maturities of Federal Housing Administration, Veterans' Administration, and conventional loans have all lengthened greatly. In addition, all types of loans showed substantial increases in typical loan-to-value ratios. The ratios of monthly loan payments and housing expense to borrower incomes remained fairly constant for FHA's, but rose substantially for VA's. Although FHA borrowers as a group held about the same relative position in the income distribution over the postwar period, loans under the VA program were increasingly made to borrowers in the relatively lower-income groups. There are no comparable time series data for conventional loans. It is to be observed that the lengthening of maturities and the rise in loan-to-value ratios that carried through 1964 were arrested and reversed in 1965–67.

Both delinquency and foreclosure experience reflected some weakening in mortgage quality in the later postwar years as compared with the remarkably strong records of the late 1940's and early 1950's. The rates of serious delinquency (i.e., loans ninety days or more in arrears) began to rise for all three classes of mortgages in 1957, although after 1961 this upward trend leveled off. Foreclosure rates remained at very low levels through about 1959, but then a steep upward trend set in which was arrested only in 1964. Our study can be viewed as an attempt to explain the trends in mortgage performance through 1963. To what extent were they attributable to the increase in refinancing and use of second mortgages, to rising loan-to-value ratios, and the other changes in loan and borrower characteristics that had taken place?

Earlier studies of these matters were deficient in several respects. The present study was formulated in the light of the earlier ones and attempted to remedy their major shortcomings. Unlike earlier studies this one used samples that were national in scope and covered conventional as well as FHA and VA mortgages. Most importantly, by using a multiple regression technique the separate effects of the various loan and borrower characteristics upon the risk of delinquency and foreclosure could be tested for statistical significance. A total of thirteen separate regressions were run to test various subsamples of loans, different clusters of independent variables, and the variables related separately to both delinquency and foreclosure. Separate samples of loans were obtained from the United States Savings and Loan League (USSLL), the Mortgage Bankers Association (MBA), and the National Association of Mutual Savings Banks (NAMSB).

The independent variables used in the analysis include: (1) loan purpose (e.g., new house purchase, refinancing); (2) the presence or absence of junior financing; (3) loan-to-value ratio; (4) loan type (i.e., FHA, VA, or conventional); (5) initial term to maturity; (6) monthly mortgage payment to borrower income ratio; (7) borrower occupation; (8) marital status; (9) number of dependents; and (10) geographic region.

The complete results of the regression analyses are presented in Chapter II. The most important ones can be summarized as follows.

Factors Related to Delinquency

1. Borrowing for *refinancing* purposes and the presence of *junior financing* appear to be the most important variables affecting the incidence of serious loan delinquency (i.e., a loan being 90 days or more in arrears).[1]

2. The *loan-to-value ratio* was found to be positively and significantly related to the probability of a loan being in delinquency status in all the equations in which this variable was tested.

3. *Term to maturity,* on the other hand, appeared to have little or no influence once the effects of other variables were removed. While the coefficient carried a negative sign in all the equations (indicating an inverse relationship to risk), it was statistically significant in only four of the six. Furthermore, the cases in which it was significant all contained fewer than the full complement of variables, indicating that this one was acting as a proxy for those we omitted. In fact, it can be observed that the more variables that were dropped the stronger this inverse relationship appeared to be. Even in our most complete specification of the equation (where the sign was still negative) we were unable to include a wealth or liquid asset variable. This may have prevented us from sufficiently isolating the effects of such things as the financial burden of the mortgage indebtedness upon the borrower. In such cases shorter terms could, in part, reflect a borrower's greater financial weakness and for that reason show higher delinquency. This would be the case, for example, if lenders demanded faster repayments from weaker (though still acceptable) borrowers, but in such an event short maturities could be said to *reflect* rather than *cause* greater risk.

4. *Occupation* turned out to be a fairly important variable. Generally speaking, professional persons, executives and managers showed the least delinquency, and self-employed persons and salesmen the most. Only slight variations were noted among the remaining occupational classes.

5. *Number of dependents* bore a significant direct relationship to delinquency risk for the USSLL sample, although in the MBA and NAMSB samples this variable was not clearly significant.

---

[1] The influence of these variables could be tested only for conventional loans, since very few FHA and VA loans are made for refinancing purposes and no secondary financing is permitted in connection with FHA and VA lending.

6. *Mortgage payment-to-borrower income ratios* were not significantly related to delinquency risk. This ostensibly surprising fact appears to be because both borrowers and lenders watch this ratio very carefully. They avoid loans in which some fairly modest critical limit is exceeded unless there is an unusual assurance that payments can be made from nonincome sources. Study showed that most loans in the samples had payment-to-income ratios below 25 per cent.

7. *Marital status* was not a statistically significant variable in any of the equations, even though the risk coefficients were uniformly lower for married than for single borrowers.

8. *Borrower age* yielded such mixed results that no generalization seems warranted, although in one sample (USSLL) borrowers under 40 appeared to be riskier than their older counterparts.

9. *Region* was included to isolate geographical influences. There were significant differences among the regions, indicating that failure to include this variable would have seriously biased the results.

10. *Loan type* was also a significant variable. While loans insured or guaranteed by the federal government have, on the whole, performed more poorly than conventionals, study showed that this differential was largely due to the variables included in the regression equations in Chapter II. Thus, *after* the influence of such variables as loan-to-value ratios, occupation, etc., had been removed, conventional loans carried *higher* risks than FHA's or VA's. Presumably, this finding reflects differences in appraisal practices and other underwriting policies for which we lacked data.

Conditional Foreclosure Risk

The second risk tested was that loans already delinquent would be foreclosed. In many cases the relationship between the various independent variables and the risk was similar to that for delinquency. The important exceptions are noted below.

1. *Term to maturity,* which was negatively related to delinquency risk, bore a direct relationship to conditional foreclosure risk.

2. *Occupation* did not prove to be a significant variable in conditional foreclosure risk, although in the USSLL data executives or managers carried a significantly higher risk coefficient than the other groups. In the MBA and NAMSB equations the salesman category carried a significantly lower one.

3. *Loan purpose* remained one of the most significant variables, but in this case new home construction as well as refinancing was a high-risk purpose.

Straight Foreclosure Risk

Straight foreclosure risk, or the risk that any given loan not currently in difficulty will end up in foreclosure, was also analyzed by the regression techniques. This analysis yielded results which could generally be inferred from an examination of delinquency and conditional foreclosure risk. That is, if a variable was positively related to both delinquency and conditional foreclosure, it was also positively related to straight foreclosure risk. If the relationship to the two earlier measured risks differed, the stronger coefficient dominated the straight foreclosure risk.

The key risk variables were once again loan purpose and junior financing. Construction loans had the highest foreclosure risk coefficient, followed closely by refinancing. Loans for home repair were next in order of risk, and the safest of all were loans for home purchase. As in all the other equations, loans involving junior financing proved to be much riskier than those that did not. Longer term to maturity as well as loan-to-value ratio was significantly and directly related to the risk that current loans would go into foreclosure.

Changes in Risks Over Time

The regression analyses just discussed provided coefficients measuring the influence on delinquency and foreclosure of several important characteristics whose incidence in the total volume of new mortgage loans was available year by year over the postwar years. By weighting these characteristics by the coefficients, indexes of risk of delinquency and foreclosure for the postwar period could be constructed. Both published and sample data were employed in developing these time series.

The variables included in one or more of the risk indexes were: (1) loan-to-value ratio, (2) term to maturity, (3) payment-to-income ratio, (4) loan purpose, and (5) junior financing. Series covering delinquency and conditional foreclosure risk were constructed for VA, FHA, and conventional loans, and a straight foreclosure risk series was constructed for conventional loans.

Although there are definite hazards in attempting to fit time series data to cross-sectional equations (see Chapter III), the time series resulting from this analysis appear to explain much of the weakening of home mortgage performance that occurred from 1957 to 1963. The study thus provides fairly convincing evidence that there was an appreciable deterioration of home mortgage quality over much of the postwar period.

Introduction and Summary

There is no question that there was a substantial increase in foreclosure risk, most of it coming in the latter part of the period.

Suggestions for Future Research

Because of the limitations of the data and methodological difficulties, we must emphasize that the conclusions arrived at in this study are tentative. While the specific limitations are dealt with at length in the text, some of the main points bear noting here.

First, there is the matter of how we have defined mortgage "quality." From some standpoints, the definition should be related to the actual losses occasioned by default or foreclosure rather than their sheer incidence. However, this approach would require data of a different sort than we had at our disposal. Our samples were drawn from "live" loans, that is, loans still on the lenders' books. What one should have in order to examine loss rates is data on terminated loans—loans whose entire history is known.

A second problem arises in conjunction with the definition of variables, both dependent and independent. The dependent variable we were seeking, namely, "quality," does not readily lend itself to quantitative measurement. Although it is possible to use, as we did, dummy classes (e.g., delinquent, or in foreclosure, for low-quality) and employ multiple regression, other techniques, such as multiple discriminant analysis, might be more appropriate to the problem. As of now, however, computational difficulties are simply too great to permit using this approach.

As to the independent variables, it seems obvious that some mixture of scalar and dummy classes is essential to meaningful analysis, but this poses serious methodological problems when using standard regression techniques. Although we followed typical practice in choosing to ignore many of these problems, the biases thus introduced may be serious.

Finally, there is the difficulty associated with applying cross-section regression coefficients to time series analysis. This application necessarily assumes that there were no material changes in variables excluded from the equations which could have caused the coefficients to behave differently. The only way to determine how stable the coefficients are, in fact, would be to make numerous cross-sectional studies. Moreover, time series data on the characteristics of outstanding as well as new loans need to be developed if adequate explanations and forecasts of the changing delinquency and foreclosure rates on outstanding loans are to be made.

Obviously, much further empirical work remains to be done on changing mortgage quality over time.

Home Mortgage Delinquency and Foreclosure

I

Background of the Study

Four conditions combined to motivate this study: (1) the large and growing importance of home mortgage [1] debt in the postwar credit structure; (2) the radical shifts that occurred, following World War II, in the characteristics of this debt; (3) the considerable rise in mortgage foreclosure and delinquency in the late 1950's and early 1960's; and (4) the lack of rigorous analysis in previous studies of the performance of home mortgage debt, so that neither the factors responsible for mortgage performance nor the degree to which mortgage quality may have changed in recent years could be assessed. This chapter deals broadly with each of these conditions.

1. The Importance of Home Mortgage Debt

A number of postwar inquiries have depicted the growing importance of residential mortgage finance in the American economy, and only a few salient facts need be cited here.[2] Earlier studies, which fo-

---

[1] Almost all of the data in this study pertain to single-family or one- to four-family housing. Mortgages on apartment and other multifamily dwellings are omitted, as are mortgages on farm dwellings. In some cases data refer to all nonfarm residential mortgages, and in a few cases some farm dwelling debt is included. In such cases the broader term "residential mortgage" is employed.

[2] Important studies of postwar developments in the real estate finance market include the following: Saul B. Klaman, *The Postwar Residential Mortgage Market,* Princeton for NBER, 1961; Raymond R. Goldsmith, Robert E. Lipsey and Morris Mendelson, *Studies in the National Balance Sheet,* Princeton for NBER, 1963; and O. Jones and L. Grebler, *The Secondary Mortgage Market,* Los Angeles: Real Estate Research Program, Univ. of California, 1961. The forthcoming study by Earley, "The Quality of Credit in the United States," provides additional background material.

cused on the depression, wartime, and immediate postwar periods, were conducted under the National Bureau's Financial Research Program.[3] Beginning in 1946, U.S. residential construction revived vigorously, following the wartime hiatus of civilian construction and more than a decade of depressed prewar house building. The entire postwar period has been one of large home building as judged by prewar standards. From 1947 through 1964, residential construction never constituted less than 29 per cent of U.S. gross domestic investment, as against typical levels of about 18 per cent prior to World War II.

Single-family housing has been the backbone of postwar American residential construction. As judged by the value of total building permits, roughly 85 per cent of new U.S. residential construction was in single-family homes in 1946, as compared with only 64 per cent in 1936. In recent years multidwelling construction has grown in relative importance, but even in 1963 single-family homes constituted 68 per cent of the value of total residential building permits. Since residential construction is peculiarly dependent on mortgage credit, almost all one-to four-family housing being bought with the aid of mortgage loans, a major sector of the American economy is thus dependent upon the performance of the home mortgage market.

As a result of the long-sustained housing boom, residential mortgage debt has grown substantially in relative importance in the U.S. debt structure. Household mortgage debt was 16 per cent of all debt (omitting the debts owed by financial institutions) in 1963, as compared with only 7 per cent in 1939. Owing to the long and lengthening maturity of home mortgages in the postwar years, the proportion of personal disposable income absorbed by payments on these mortgages remained fairly small. But it was not negligible, being 3.5 per cent in 1963, more than twice its level in 1945.

The American financial system has become more dependent on the quality of home mortgage debt than ever before. Savings and loan associations, America's fastest-growing major type of financial institution in the postwar years, are of course especially heavily involved; almost 84 per cent of their total assets was invested in nonfarm residential mortgages at the end of 1963. Other types of institutions have increased their holdings of mortgages sharply. More than two-thirds of the funds of mutual savings banks were so invested in 1963, as compared with only about one-third before World War II. Less than 10 per cent of

---

[3] For a summary of these studies, see J. E. Morton, *Urban Mortgage Lending: Comparative Markets and Experience,* Princeton for NBER, 1956.

the total assets of life insurance companies was invested in residential mortgages as late as 1948, but more than 20 per cent was so employed in 1963. Even commercial banks, whose investment in residential mortgages comprised only about 4 per cent of total assets before World War II had 8 per cent so invested at the end of 1963. Lack of up-to-date over-all data makes it impossible to estimate the proportion of the total assets of all U.S. financial institutions combined that now consist of residential mortgages; but by 1958, national balance sheet data put this figure at 16 per cent, more than twice its prewar level. Judging by later partial data for the major types of institutional holders, this probably approached 20 per cent by 1963. The stake of the American credit system in the quality of home mortgage debt is thus large.

One of the significant postwar developments in home mortgage finance has been the increased importance of financial institutions relative to other lenders. The four major lenders—savings and loan associations, mutual savings banks, life insurance companies, and commercial banks—together held about 86 per cent of the mortgages outstanding on one- to four-family properties at the end of 1963, as compared with only 65 per cent in 1930 and 59 per cent in 1940. The most dramatic growth was in the savings and loan sector. Savings and loan associations accounted for about 44 per cent of total holdings of home mortgages in 1963–64, as against only 22.5 per cent at the end of 1940. Mutual savings banks, life insurance companies and commercial banks are now of roughly equal quantitative importance, each accounting for about 15 per cent of total holdings of one- to four-family mortgages in 1963–64. Their shares had grown slightly as compared with prewar years.

Owing to the rapid growth of mortgage banking, the pattern of the origination of mortgage loans has come to diverge substantially from the pattern of their holdings. Mortgage bankers generate and issue mortgages, but typically sell them to other institutional investors, especially savings banks and life insurance companies. Mortgage bankers also frequently service the loans, collecting instalments and otherwise dealing with borrowers. Before the war, in 1940, mortgage companies originated roughly 15 per cent of new one- to four-family home mortgages; by 1960, this proportion had reached 19 per cent of a vastly greater volume of lending.

Mortgage banking is especially prevalent in financing operations under government-sponsored FHA and VA programs. They originated about a fourth of new FHA loans in 1946 and a half in 1960. In 1960,

55 per cent of new one- to four-family VA mortgages were made by mortgage bankers.

The over-all composition of home mortgages among conventional, FHA-insured, and VA-guaranteed loans is relevant to their quality, although the relevance is likely to be exaggerated. In the earlier postwar years, the government-sponsored fraction of new mortgages was substantial, but in no year did the conventional loan fraction fall much below two-thirds, and it remained between 75 and 80 per cent in the early 1960's. In 1963 roughly 64 per cent of the one- to four-family mortgage debt outstanding was in conventional loans without government guarantee. In recent years the private insurance of conventional mortgages has spread. By 1964 between $1.5 and $2 billion worth of insurance was in force on conventional mortgages. The insurance, which is only written on loans having loan-to-value ratios in excess of 80 per cent, covered less than 1 per cent of the outstanding one- to four-family mortgage debt. It is not likely that substantial changes in the proportion of loans privately insured will take place in the near future.

In any case, the significance of insurance and guarantees for the quality of over-all mortgage debt is not great. Private mortgage insurance could not stand up for long against a serious rise in foreclosures. Even lending on government-insured or -guaranteed mortgages would be inhibited if delinquency and foreclosure became epidemic, and both the demand for and construction of housing would fall off under such conditions, with serious economic consequences.

2. Changing Mortgage Characteristics

TERMS

The postwar years brought about a revolution in the terms of home mortgage loans in America. Changes were particularly great in the length of maturities and in loan-to-value ratios. The VA and FHA programs produced excellent statistics on these terms, and representative terms for conventional mortgages have been collected since about 1950 by the U.S. Savings and Loan League and the Federal Home Loan Bank Board. There are also reasonably satisfactory statistics on the course of the typical relationship between the payments called for under FHA and VA mortgages and the income of the mortgagors. These are the three terms, in addition to the contract interest rate, included in the sample data used in this study.[4]

[4] A fourth important variable, the accuracy of the appraisal underlying the loan-to-value ratio, is unfortunately almost never ascertainable from lenders' rec-

Table 1 and Chart 1 show the upward trend in the average maturities of newly written FHA, VA and conventional loans on home properties from 1946 through 1967. With the exception of the years centering around the Korean crisis, average maturities rose almost every year through 1965 when the trend was arrested.

By 1960, the thirty-year FHA loan, first authorized in 1954, had become typical. (Thirty-five-year maturities were later authorized in some cases.) The average maturity of single-family FHA mortgages on new homes rose to thirty-one years in 1963, the year for which the performance data in the present study were secured. By that time even FHA loans on existing homes had risen to an average maturity of more than twenty-eight years. The average maturity of VA loans, like that of FHA's, continued to rise year by year (with the exception of the Korean period) through 1965. A thirty-year maturity became typical on new-home loans in the early 1960's, compared with less than twenty years at the beginning of the VA program after World War II. The proportional increase in maturities on loans financing the purchase of existing homes was comparable.

After the war, the typical maturity of conventional mortgages was, as before, considerably shorter than that of FHA and VA loans. Proportionately, however, their maturities increased even more sharply, especially after the mid-1950's. Even for the first few years after the war, conventional loans of less than fifteen years on new homes were typical. But by 1963 the median maturity of conventional loans made by savings and loan associations was almost twenty-four years for new homes and twenty-one for loans for the purchase of existing dwellings. In the case of conventionals, typical maturities continued to rise slightly even through 1967.

The sharp rise in typical loan-to-value ratios has been as significant as the lengthening of maturities. Summary data appear in Table 2 and Chart 2.

The VA program led the field in the move toward very low margin mortgages. No down payments were required initially on standard VA home mortgage loans. Down payments varying with the size of loan were imposed in 1950, revoked in April 1953, reimposed in July 1955, and revoked again in April 1958. There have been no VA down payment

ords. Other terms, such as technical provisions regarding foreclosure, prepayment privileges, and special covenants, have also had to be omitted for lack of data. The contract interest rate was included as a variable in the cross-section analysis, but its movements through time were so clearly dominated by changing monetary and credit conditions, rather than by quality shifts, that the movements are not noted here.

TABLE 1
Postwar Trends in Home Mortgage Maturities, 1946-67
(years)

| | Average Maturity of New Loans | | | | Estimated Median Maturity of New Loans[a] | |
| | FHA Single-Family Homes (Section 203) | | VA Primary Loans (Section 501) | | Conventional Loans by Savings and Loan Associations | |
Year	New Homes (1)	Existing Homes (2)	New Homes (3)	Existing Homes (4)	New Homes (5)	Existing Homes (6)
1946	21.0	18.9	19.8	18.2	n.a.	n.a.
1947	20.2	19.1	20.2	16.7	n.a.	n.a.
1948	20.1	19.3	19.7	16.1	n.a.	n.a.
1949	22.8	19.8	21.2	17.4	n.a.	n.a.
1950	24.1	20.2	23.1	19.7	14.3	12.3
1951[b]	23.4	21.1	24.0	18.2	16.2	13.6
1952[b]	21.7	19.7	23.1	18.7	16.3	13.9
1953	22.2	19.9	23.2	19.3	16.5	13.9
1954	22.9	20.1	25.9	21.4	16.7	14.6
1955	25.6	22.7	27.4	22.4	17.4	15.1
1956	25.5	22.5	27.2	22.0	17.5	15.1
1957	25.5	22.5	27.3	21.3	18.5	15.2
1958	27.3	24.2	28.3	22.3	19.8	15.5
1959	28.8	25.1	28.9	23.6	21.1	16.1
1960	29.2	25.8	28.9	23.6	21.7	16.5
1961	29.5	26.7	29.1	25.4	21.9	16.9
1962	30.3	27.4	29.2	26.6	22.7	18.8
1963	31.0	27.9	29.3	27.3	23.9	20.2
1964	31.4	28.4	29.3	27.7	24.6	20.9
1965	31.7	28.6	29.4	27.8	25.3	22.2
1966	30.3	28.4	29.4	27.8	25.0	22.2
1967	29.8	28.5	29.4	28.0	25.4	23.1

SOURCE: For FHA, HHFA *Annual Reports* and *Quarterly Reports on FHA Trends;* VA data supplied by Veterans' Administration; conventional loan data supplied by U.S. Savings and Loan League.

[a]Medians are estimated from frequency distributions of "most typical" maturities reported by a large sample of savings and loan associations in the spring of each year.

[b]Selective government controls over maximum maturities were in effect in most months of 1951 and 1952.

n.a. = not available.

CHART 1

Postwar Trends in Home Mortgage Maturities, 1946–67

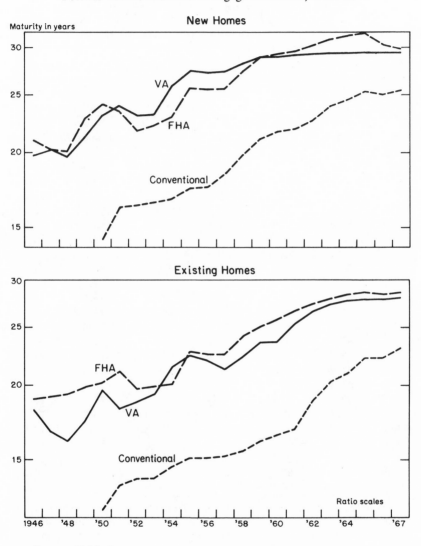

SOURCE: Table 1.

TABLE 2

Postwar Trends in Home Mortgage Loan-to-Value Ratios, 1946-67
(per cent)

| Year | Average Loan-to-Value Ratios of New Loans | | | | Estimated Median Loan-to-Purchase-Price Ratio[a] | |
| | FHA Single-Family Homes (Section 203) | | VA Primary Loans (Section 501) | | Conventional Loans Made by Savings and Loan Associations | |
	New Homes (1)	Existing Homes (2)	New Homes (3)	Existing Homes (4)	New Homes (5)	Existing Homes (6)
1946	84.1	78.6	92.7	89.1	n.a.	n.a.
1947	81.2	77.3	90.7	89.2	n.a.	n.a.
1948	80.1	76.5	84.5	83.8	n.a.	n.a.
1949	83.6	76.6	86.5	84.6	n.a.	n.a.
1950	85.0	76.4	91.9	86.4	69.2	64.6
1951[b]	82.5	73.6	89.6	80.7	65.5	63.6
1952[b]	80.4	76.1	86.9	80.3	67.0	64.1
1953	82.9	77.5	88.8	82.0	67.0	63.9
1954	82.2	77.8	92.6	86.8	68.3	65.2
1955	85.0	82.2	94.5	88.4	71.6	67.9
1956	83.2	80.3	93.1	86.3	71.6	67.9
1957	82.3	82.5	92.2	85.8	71.3	67.3
1958	88.7	88.1	94.3	87.4	72.7	68.9
1959	91.0	89.7	96.7	89.0	74.4	71.1
1960	91.4	90.5	96.8	90.7	75.3	72.0
1961	92.2	91.4	97.7	92.5	75.7	73.1
1962	92.7	92.1	97.8	94.9	76.6	75.1
1963	92.7	92.5	97.6	95.8	77.0	75.6
1964	92.9	92.8	97.6	96.2	80.4	76.1
1965	92.7	92.7	97.2	96.2	76.6[c]	75.3[c]
1966	92.7	93.0	97.3	96.8	75.7[c]	74.5[c]
1967	92.4	93.0	97.5	97.6	75.8[c]	75.2[c]

SOURCE: For FHA, HHFA *Annual Reports* and *Quarterly Reports on FHA Trends;* VA data supplied by Veterans' Administration; conventional loan data from 1950 through 1964 supplied by U.S. Savings and Loan League, for 1965-67 data see note c below.

[a]Medians are estimated from frequency distribution of "most typical" loan-to-purchase price ratios reported by a large sample of associations in the spring of each year. The ratios are for loans on

CHART 2

Postwar Trends in Home Mortgage Loan-to-Value Ratios, 1947–67

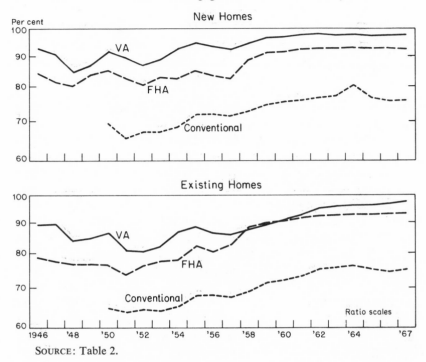

SOURCE: Table 2.

requirements since that time, although the practices of including closing costs in the mortgage amount—the making of "no no-down-payment loans"—is no longer permitted. As Table 2 shows, by 1963 the average loan-to-value ratio on VA new homes was almost 98 per cent and the average ratio on VA loans for the purchase of existing homes was only slightly lower. Thereafter the rise in loan ratios on new homes ceased although those on existing homes continued to rise slightly.

---

the following price groups of houses: 1950, unspecified; 1951, $9,000-$15,000; 1952–54, $10,000-$15,000; 1955-64, under $15,000.

[b]Government controls over maximum loan-to-value ratios were in effect during most months of 1951 and 1952.

[c]1965-67 data are averages as published by the Federal Home Loan Bank Board. They are not strictly comparable with earlier figures.

n.a. = not available.

Restrictions on the proportions of property value that could be advanced on FHA home mortgages were successively relaxed during the postwar years. Average loan-to-value ratios on new loans remained quite moderate through the mid-1950's, but thereafter began to rise rapidly. In 1963, FHA regulations permitted mortgages of up to 97 per cent of appraised value on the first $15,000, 90 per cent on the next $5,000, and 75 per cent on any remaining value up to a maximum loan of $30,000. The actual average loan-to-value ratios in 1963 were above 92 per cent on both new and existing home loans. Thereafter there was little change through 1967. The proportionate rise in loan-to-value ratios over the postwar years was even greater for FHA than for VA loans, as the chart shows. It is also significant that the earlier substantial difference between loan-to-value ratios for FHA loans on new and existing homes had disappeared by the early 1960's.

The main effective limits on the loan-to-value ratios of conventional home mortgages have been restrictions on the lending powers of federal and state chartered savings and loan associations which have membership in the Federal Home Loan Bank System. Before the war these were permitted to loan only up to 60 per cent of the appraised value of home properties. This limit was raised, subject to certain limitations, to 75 per cent, and later to 80 per cent, during the 1950's. In 1958, federal savings and loan associations were permitted in certain cases to loan up to 90 per cent of the appraised value of homes. Although typical loan-to-purchase price ratios remain lower for conventional than for government-sponsored mortgages, the uptrend has been proportionally about as great, as Chart 2 reveals. In 1964 the estimated median loan-to-purchase price ratio of loans reported by members of the U.S. Savings and Loan League was 80 per cent for new construction loans and 76 per cent for the purchase of existing homes, much above their levels in the early 1950's. Later data were not strictly comparable, but it appears there was a slight drop after 1964.

The postwar American housing market has been a market for new homes to a greater extent than before the war. Both government-sponsored and conventional mortgage finance have been directed especially toward new housing, much of it in large tracts and subdivisions. To some extent the markets for new and existing housing have been somewhat separate, perhaps more so than before the war. As the charts show, however, the pronounced easing of terms has characterized both markets. It remains normal to lend for somewhat shorter periods and at lower loan-to-value ratios on existing homes than on new ones, but the easing of terms on the former has been, on the whole, even more pronounced. Over the period for which the loans included in our study were contracted, the very long-term, low-margin home mortgage was typical for all types of loans and lenders and in all parts of the country. We will examine the effects of these terms on loan performance in later chapters.

LOAN PAYMENT-TO-INCOME RATIOS

One of the relationships that has become more important to quality with the growth of long-maturity, low down payment loans is the percentage of the monthly mortgage payment (or estimated total housing expense) to the income of the borrower. It is interesting to look at the trend of this percentage on typical loans over the postwar years.

Unfortunately, there are no representative time series for conventional loans. Data for VA loans are available from 1954 on. FHA data are available for 1940 and each of the years 1946 to the present. Table 3 and Chart 3 present these data.

For FHA loans the notable feature is the stability of these percentages, both for new and existing home loans. The average percentage of borrower income absorbed by mortgage payment on loans for new homes did not exceed the level of 1940 in any postwar year. The low point in the percentage occurred in the mid-1950's. Since then it has risen somewhat, but it remained moderate in 1963 as compared with either the prewar or immediate postwar years and dropped slightly after 1963. The situation is broadly similar for FHA loans on existing homes.

In the case of VA loans, the situation is not so favorable. Satisfactory data are available only back to 1956 and only for the percentage of average total housing expense to average borrower income on loans on both new and existing homes combined. But these show a considerable weakening in this relationship between 1954 and 1967. The average ratio of income to housing expense was only 22 per cent in 1956, rose to 29 per cent in 1963 and to 30 per cent in 1966. Since these data are based on after-tax rather than pre-tax income, they are not comparable with the FHA data but the disparity in movement in the late 1950's and early 1960's was notable.

3. Trends in Borrower Characteristics

The lengthening of maturities and the rise in loan-to-value ratios have naturally increased the importance of borrower characteristics to the quality of home mortgages. Borrower characteristics available here include income, occupation, marital status, number of dependents, and

TABLE 3

*Average Percentages of Mortgage Payment and Total Housing
Expense to Borrower Income, FHA and VA Home Mortgage Loans*
(per cent)

	FHA Single-Family Home Loans (Section 203)				VA Prior-Approval Loans, New and Existing Homes Combined (Section 501)
	New Homes		Existing Homes		
Year	Average Mortgage Payment (1)	Total Housing Expense^a (2)	Average Mortgage Payment (3)	Total Housing Expense^a (4)	Total Housing Expense to After-Tax Income (5)
1940	17	n.a.	15	n.a.	n.a.
1946	15	21	14	20	n.a.
1947	16	22	14	20	n.a.
1948	16	22	14	20	n.a.
1949	16	22	15	20	n.a.
1950	16	22	15	20	n.a.
1951	15	20	14	19	n.a.
1952	15	20	14	19	n.a.
1953	15	20	15	19	n.a.
1954	15	20	15	19	n.a.
1955	15	20	15	19	n.a.
1956	15	19	15	19	22
1957	15	20	15	20	24
1958	16	20	16	20	25
1959	16	20	16	20	26
1960	17	21	16	21	26
1961	17	21	16	20	28
1962	17	21	16	20	28
1963	17	21	16	20	29
1964	17	21	16	21	29
1965	16	21	16	21	29
1966	16	21	16	21	30
1967	16	21	16	21	30

SOURCE: FHA percentages for 1940-64 computed from data in
Annual Reports of the FHA and HHFA; 1965-67 data from *FHA Trends*.
VA percentages computed from data in *VA Loan Guarantee Highlights*.
Since they are based on after-tax income they are properly comparable
to FHA data, but the uptrend from 1956 on is the significant comparison.

^{a}The sum of mortgage payments, expenses for heating and utilities,
and FHA-estimated cost of maintenance and repair.

n.a. = not available.

CHART 3

Postwar Trends in Housing Expense to Borrower Income Ratios, FHA and
VA Home Mortgages, 1946–67

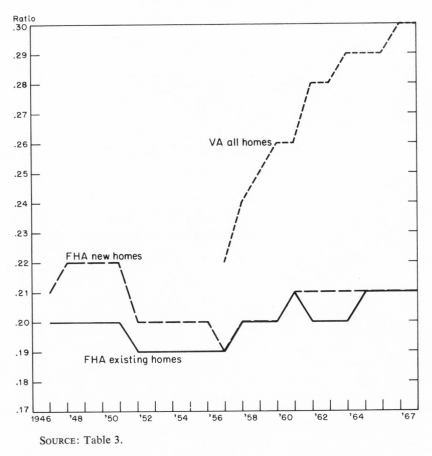

SOURCE: Table 3.

age. It is of interest to survey briefly the information available on the trends of these variables among home mortgage borrowers generally over the postwar years. The data are far from adequate, but some significant trends are observable.

BORROWER INCOME

Higher income is normally associated with a lower proportion of income absorbed in housing expense, which thus increases the cushion available to take care of mortgage and other obligations. Higher incomes are also normally associated with greater wealth and liquid asset holdings, as well as with favorable occupational status. Hence the postwar trend of mortgage borrower incomes, both absolutely and relative to incomes of the entire population, is worth noting.

The rising incomes of the U.S. population since World War II, in both money and real terms, have unquestionably been an important factor in maintaining home mortgage performance. Mortgage borrowers, generally, have higher than average incomes. The following data are significant primarily in that they show whether mortgage borrowers have come to be drawn from relatively higher sectors of the family income structure over the course of the postwar years.

Table 4 shows the course of the average effective monthly income of FHA Section 203 borrowers and the ratio of this income to the median nonfarm family income of the United States. Table 5 presents similar data for VA borrowers. Chart 4 illustrates the behavior of the ratios for both FHA and VA borrowers.

FHA borrowers on both new and existing homes have considerably higher than median income, and until the mid-1950's this favorable relative income position improved. For new home borrowers the ratio improved through 1957; for existing home borrowers it reached its strongest position somewhat earlier. From 1957 on the trend became downward in both cases, however. In 1963–64 the average income of FHA borrowers relative to the population at large appears to have been about what it was shortly after the war.

The average income of VA borrowers, on the other hand, has had an unfavorable trend relative to median U.S. family income over the period for which data are available. In 1954 the average income of VA borrowers was about 30 per cent above the U.S. median, thus comparing favorably with FHA borrowers. By 1963, however, the VA average was very little higher than the median. There is some evidence here of a weakening of the quality of VA mortgage loans. It should be observed, however, that VA loans were declining in relative importance over these years.

There are unfortunately no good data on the postwar movements of the average incomes of conventional mortgagors, who owe much the larger portion of aggregate home mortgage debt. Fortunately, Survey Research Center data, based on representative samples of American spending units, can provide essential trends for all classes of mortgage borrowers combined, including conventional loan mortgagors. This evidence indicates that mortgage borrowers generally have more than shared in the postwar rise in money and real income. Although the data

TABLE 4

Postwar Trends in Average Income Levels of New FHA (Section
203) Borrowers and Ratios to Median Incomes of Nonfarm Families

Year	Average Effective Monthly Income (before taxes)[a]		Ratio to Median Nonfarm Family Income	
	New-Home Borrowers (1)	Existing-Home Borrowers (2)	New-Home Borrowers (3)	Existing-Home Borrowers (4)
1940	$222	$251	n.a.	n.a.
1946	302	303	1.21	1.21
1947	331	328	1.24	1.23
1948	367	359	1.30	1.27
1949	357	395	1.29	1.43
1950	351	403	1.21	1.38
1951	388	431	1.19	1.32
1952	430	452	1.25	1.32
1953	440	495	1.18	1.33
1954	469	520	1.27	1.42
1955	497	518	1.27	1.32
1956	545	549	1.29	1.30
1957	593	571	1.36	1.31
1958	601	581	1.35[b]	1.31[b]
1959	610	592	1.29	1.25
1960	632	605	1.31	1.25
1961	645	621	1.31	1.26
1962	641	636	1.26	1.25
1963	666	648	1.24	1.21
1964	677	656	1.20	1.16

SOURCE: Col. 1 and 2: 1940 from *Annual Report* of FHA, 1940
Table 47, p. 84; 1946 from *Annual Report* of National Housing Agency,
1946, pp. 156, 158; 1947-60 from *Annual Reports* of HHFA; 1961-64
from *FHA Trends,* various quarterly dates. Median nonfarm income
data are from *Current Population Reports,* Series P-60, U.S. Department of Commerce.

[a]FHA-estimated amount of the "mortgagor's earning capacity . . .
likely to prevail during approximately the first third of mortgage
term."

[b]1959 nonfarm median income was missing from source. Ratio was
estimated from the median for all families by adjusting for the 1958
ratio of nonfarm to all-family medians.

n.a. = not available.

TABLE 5

Postwar Trends in Average Income Levels of New VA
Mortgage Borrowers and Ratios to Median Income of
Nonfarm Families, Prior-Approval Primary Loans
Under Section 501, 1954-63

(new and existing homes combined)

Year	Estimated Mortgagor Average Monthly Income (before taxes) (1)	Ratio to Median Nonfarm Family Income (2)
1954	$481	1.31
1955	501	1.28
1956	528	1.25
1957	540	1.24
1958	545	1.23
1959	531	1.12[a]
1960	560	1.09
1961	522	1.06
1962	530	1.04
1963	546	1.02

SOURCE: Col. 1, based on data supplied by Veterans' Administration. These data stated income after taxes, but equivalent before-tax figures were estimated for this purpose. Median nonfarm income underlying col. 2 from *Current Population Reports*.

[a]See Table 4, note b.

have rather wide sampling errors, the trends are so strong as to be convincing.

The data are summarized in Table 6. The top panel of the table shows that homeownership is most prevalent in the upper-income quintiles of the population, and in these quintiles the incidence of home-ownership increased most from 1949 to 1960. Since the bulk of home-owners, especially those acquiring homes for the first time, are mortgage debtors, this is strong evidence of a greater upward movement in the family income of home mortgagors than of the population as a whole between these years.

The lower panels of the table, which cover home mortgage debtors only, tend to confirm this conclusion, although the data unfortunately go back only to 1958. Between 1958 and 1963, Panel B shows, the over-all percentage of nonfarm homeowning families with mortgage indebtedness rose only slightly, but the percentages in the higher-income groups rose markedly and in most lower-income groups the percentage

CHART 4

Ratio of Average Income of FHA and VA Mortgage Borrowers to Median Family Income, 1946–64

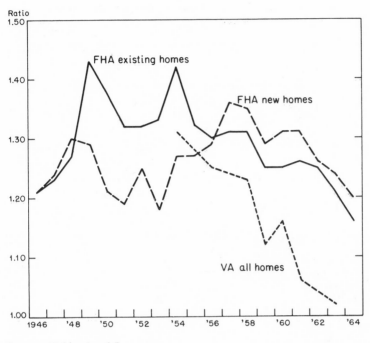

SOURCE: Tables 4 and 5.

fell. The same conclusion can be inferred from Panel C. The estimated share of total mortgage debt owed by families whose incomes were $10,000 or more rose sharply, from 21 per cent in 1958 to 38 per cent in 1963. Between these years only a small part of these changes could be attributed to rising money incomes and shifting income composition among the population.

In sum, it seems clear that those who owed residential mortgage debt enjoyed increases in income considerably greater than the average American family over the postwar years. This must have been an important factor in maintaining the quality of home mortgages.

OCCUPATIONAL COMPOSITION

There are no available time series on the occupational distribution of home mortgagors. Even cross-section information is scanty. It is, however, possible to draw inferences from the changing homeownership patterns of different occupational classes, owing to the very high correla-

TABLE 6

Postwar Changes in the Income Composition of
Homeowners and Residential Mortgage Debtors
(per cent)

A. *Nonfarm Families Owing Homes, by Income Quintiles, 1949-60*

Quintile	1949	1954	1960	Change, 1949-60
Lowest	40	45	42	+ 2
Second	43	46	47	+ 4
Third	47	51	55	+ 8
Fourth	55	65	68	+ 13
Highest	69	71	77	+ 8
All families	51	56	58	+ 7

B. *Nonfarm Homeowning Families With Mortgage Debt,*
by Income Groups, 1958-63

1962 Family Income	1958	1960	1963	Change, 1958-63
Under $3,000	22	24	25	+ 3
$3,000-4,999	52	54	45	- 7
$5,000-5,999	65	66	59	- 6
$6,000-7,499	74	72	74	0
$7,500-9,999	72	70	72	0
$10,000-14,999	68	78	70	+ 2
$15,000 and over	52	68	72	+ 20
All families	56	60	59	+ 3

C. *Total Mortgage Debt Owed by Income Groups in Panel B*

1962 Family Income	1958	1960	1963	Change, 1958-63
Under $3,000	4	4	3	- 1
$3,000-4,999	12	12	9	- 3
$5,000-5,999	13	12	8	- 5
$6,000-7,499	25	19	18	- 7
$7,500-9,999	25	20	24	- 1
$10,000-14,999	15	21	25	+ 10
$15,000 and over	6	12	13	+ 7
All families	100	100	100	

SOURCE: Survey Research Center, *Survey of Consumer Finances,*
Ann Arbor, Mich.: panel A, *1960,* p. 60; panels B and C, *1963,* p. 87.

TABLE 7

Postwar Changes in Homeownership by Occupational Class, 1949-63

(per cent of all nonfarm families owning homes)

Occupation of Family Head	1949	1954	1960	1963	Change, 1949-63
Professional	48	58	58	62	+14
Managerial		59		72	+13[a]
	66		75	79[b]	+13
Self-employed		76		85	+ 9
Clerical and sales	46	55	59	66	+20
Skilled			64	69	+ 5[c]
	52	54		62[d]	+10
Semiskilled			58	56	- 2[c]
Unskilled and service	46	41	39	42	- 4
All families	51	56	58	61	+10

SOURCE: *1960 Survey of Consumer Finances*, p. 60; *1963*, pp. 90-91.

[a] 1954-63.

[b] A weighted average of "managers, officials" and "self-employed businessmen, artisans" in accordance with their relative numbers in *1963 Survey of Consumer Finances*, Table 5-6, p. 91. The percentages given for each separate category are listed above, along with their weighted averages.

[c] 1960-63.

[d] A weighted average of "craftsmen, foremen" and "operatives" in accordance with their relative numbers, *ibid.*

tion between homeowning and mortgage owing, and the known upward movement of the population towards occupations of higher skills. Estimates of the occupational distribution of homeowners between 1949 and 1963 are shown in Table 7. Chart 5 illustrates the changes occurring between 1949 and 1963.

The largest proportionate increase occurred in the clerical and sales group. Increases were substantial also in the professional and self-employed groups. On the other hand, the percentage of homeownership among unskilled and service workers actually decreased.

AGE, MARITAL STATUS, AND DEPENDENTS

There are almost no good data on the marital status or the number of dependents of postwar home mortgage borrowers, although it is known

CHART 5

Percentage of Nonfarm Families Owning Homes, by Occupation of Family
Head, 1949 and 1963

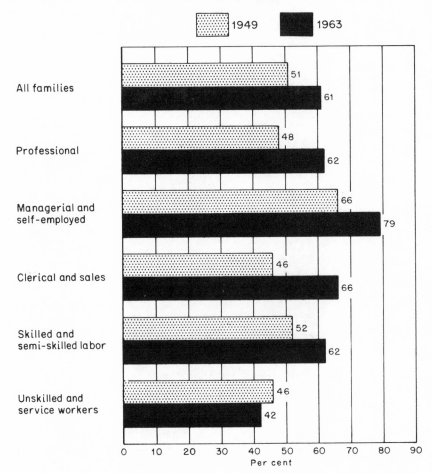

SOURCE: Table 7.

that they are somewhat concentrated in the younger married groups
with increasing numbers of children. Some data suggestive of the changing age composition of homeowners and mortgage debtors are summarized in Table 8.

It appears from these data that the concentration of mortgage debt
among the younger age groups has decreased considerably since 1949.

The sharpest increase in homeowning between 1949 and 1963, it would appear, was in the age groups from 35 to 54 years; the largest rise in the incidence of mortgage indebtedness between 1958 and 1963 was in the 45–54 age group. The share of total mortgage debt owed by household heads in both the 18–35 and 35–44 age groups decreased between these latter years. It would thus appear that there was some shift, over

TABLE 8

Postwar Changes in Homeownership and Mortgage Debt by
Various Age Groups, 1949-63

(per cent, by age of family head)

A. All Nonfarm Families Owning Homes

Age	1949	1954	1960	1963	Change, 1949-63
18–24	21	17	14	15	−6
25–34	35	42	44	47	+ 12
35–44	53	57	64	71	+ 18
45–54	59	63	69	72	+ 13
55–64	62	66	62	63	+ 1
65 and over	59	63	65	72	+ 13

B. Homeowning Families with Mortgage Debt

Age	1958	1960	1963	Change, 1958-63
18–35	84	85	84	0
35–44	74	81	79	+ 5
45–54	54	62	65	+ 11
55–64	33	36	43	+ 10
65 and over	18	17	18	0

C. Total Mortgage Debt

Age	1958	1960	1963	Change, 1958-63
18–35	31	30	27	−4
35–44	39	37	36	−3
45–54	19	23	26	+ 7
55–64	7	7	8	+ 1
65 and over	4	3	3	−1

SOURCE: *1960 Survey of Consumer Finances*, p. 60; *1963*, pp. 87, 90-91.

the postwar years, toward a larger share of home mortgage debt in the middle-aged group.

4. The Postwar Trend of Mortgage Performance

For a number of years after World War II, the performance of this growing mass of home mortgages was remarkably strong. The brisk demand for housing and the generally rising prices of residential land and structures, combined with the rise of money and real income and the stability of employment, meant that mortgage payments were well maintained and that even those properties on which payments faltered could readily be sold at prices sufficient to satisfy indebtedness. It was only in the late 1950's that these conditions weakened and delinquency and foreclosures began to rise.

FORECLOSURES

Table 9 and Chart 6 present data on annual rates of mortgage foreclosures from 1950 through 1967. Data for the several types of mortgage are not exactly comparable, but the broad comparisons and trends are reasonably representative.

Although few comparable prewar rates are available, it is known that the rates of foreclosure on residential mortgages during the early and mid-1950's were extremely low by historical standards. It was not until 1960 that foreclosure rates rose appreciably, and only in 1961 were the increases substantial. From 1962 through 1965, foreclosure rates continued to rise, although the increases moderated in 1964 and 1965 and dropped slightly thereafter.

During the 1950's, foreclosure rates on VA, FHA and conventional mortgages did not diverge greatly. In the early 1960's, however, rates on VA loans rose appreciably faster than those on conventionals, and rates on FHA's rose especially rapidly. By 1963, foreclosure rates on VA loans were more than twice as high as estimated rates on conventionals, and rates on FHA loans were roughly four times as high. Unfortunately there are no really satisfactory data for conventionals beyond 1963.[5]

---

[5] The foreclosure data for conventional mortgages generally are not very satisfactory. The Federal Home Loan Bank Board estimates for all conventional one- to four-family mortgaged dwellings shown in Table 9 extend only through 1963, and in that year the rate indicated was much below that derived from data covering all insured savings and loan associations, which first became available in 1963. In that year this latter rate (which, however, includes voluntary transfers of deeds in lieu of foreclosure as well as foreclosures proper) was 5.04 per 1,000 loans, as compared with the rate of 2.48 estimated for all conventional loans. The

TABLE 9

Postwar Nonfarm Mortgage Foreclosure Rates, 1950-67

(per 1,000 mortgaged units)

Year	All Nonfarm Real Estate (1)	Conventional Mortgages (2)	FHA Mortgages (3)	VA Mortgages (4)
1950	2.17	1.60	2.00	2.92
1951	1.67	1.53	1.01	1.33
1952	1.55	1.49	.89	1.11
1953	1.70	1.84	.63	.98
1954	1.93	1.97	1.77	1.04
1955	1.94	1.98	2.00	1.24
1956	1.97	1.88	2.46	1.53
1957	2.08	2.15	1.53	1.78
1958	2.46	2.60	1.34	2.31
1959	2.44	2.33	2.03	2.75
1960	2.71	2.48	3.25	2.86
1961	3.70	2.77	6.70	4.19
1962	4.18	2.31	9.65	5.75
1963	4.52	2.48	10.89	6.24
1964	4.79	n.a.	11.80	6.85
1965	4.93	n.a.	12.08	6.60
1966	4.81	n.a.	12.03	6.46
1967	4.38	n.a.	9.93	5.44

SOURCE: Col. 1, Federal Home Loan Bank Board, revised series, 1965. Based on all mortgaged structures. From *Housing and Urban Development Trends,* (U.S.D.H.U.D.) Annual data, May 1968, Table A-57. Col. 2, an earlier FHLBB series based on samples of one- to four-family mortgaged units. From *Savings and Loan Fact Book,* 1964, Table 65, p. 78. Cols. 3 and 4, *from Housing and Urban Development Trends,* Table A-58, based on FHA and VA data.

n.a. = not available.

The most notable feature of the table and chart, however, is the upward trend, between the mid-1950's and the mid-1960's, in all four measures of home mortgage mortality. Foreclosure rates rose somewhat

insured savings and loan association rate rose to 5.30 in 1964 and to 5.70 in 1965. Inasmuch as almost all home mortgages held by savings and loan associations are conventional loans, these rates should be reasonably representative for savings-and-loan-held conventional mortgages, and it would appear reasonable to compare these rates, rather than the lower rates shown for conventionals in Table 9, with rates for FHA's and VA's.

CHART 6

Postwar Nonfarm Mortgage Foreclosure Rates, 1950–67

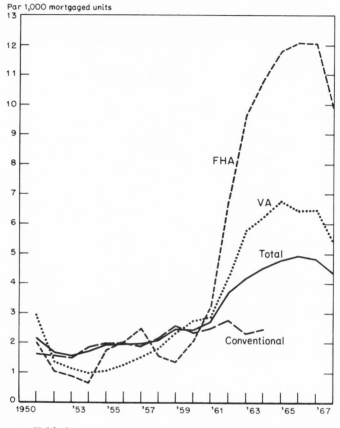

SOURCE: Table 9.

more steeply during recession years, but rose also in years of prosperity. Even the years of sustained prosperity following 1960 did not arrest their upward trend until 1966.

DELINQUENCY

The most sensitive data on the postwar preformance of home mortgages are the quarterly delinquency statistics gathered by the leading associations of mortgage lenders. The U.S. Savings and Loan League, the Mortgage Bankers Association, the National Association of Mutual Savings Banks and the Life Insurance Association of America began to gather such statistics in the early 1950's. Their quarterly movements are indicated in Chart 7, and the annual averages are summarized in Table 10. The relative levels of rates for the four associations should not be too

CHART 7

Nonfarm Home Mortgage Delinquency Rates Reported by Important Classes of Lenders, 1952–68

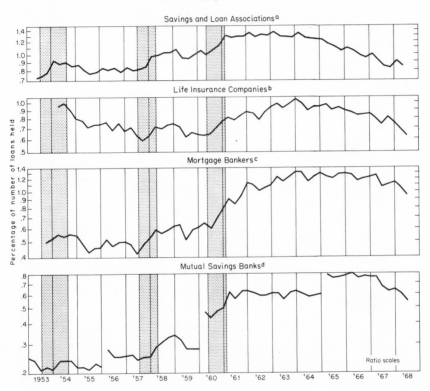

SOURCE: See source for Table 10.

NOTE: Shaded areas represent business cycle contractions; unshaded areas, expansions (monthly chronology).

a Loans two months or more delinquent, as reported to U.S. Savings and Loan League.

b All city loans (not exclusively one- to four-family housing loans) two months or more delinquent, as reported to the Life Insurance Association of America.

c One- to four-family housing loans two months or more delinquent (including loans in foreclosure), as reported to the Mortgage Bankers Association of America.

d Loans three months or more delinquent, as reported to the National Association of Mutual Savings Banks. Loans in foreclosure are included beginning with 1956. Beginning with 1960, reports cover only one- to four-family housing loans.

TABLE 10

Nonfarm Residential Mortgage Delinquency Rates[a] Reported by Important Classes of Lenders, 1953-67
(percentage of number of loans held)

Year	Savings and Loan Associations (1)	Life Insurance Companies (2)	Mortgage Bankers (3)	Mutual Savings Banks (4)
1953	0.75[b]	n.a.	0.51[c]	0.22[d]
1954	0.89	0.92	0.55	0.24[d]
1955	0.80	0.74	0.46	0.22[d]
1956	0.81	0.72	0.50	0.26
1957	0.82	0.64	0.48	0.25
1958	1.01	0.72	0.59	0.32
1959	0.99	0.66	0.58	0.29
1960	1.06	0.68	0.68	0.47[e]
1961	1.29	0.82	0.95	0.61[e]
1962	1.32	0.86	1.06	0.60[e]
1963	1.31	0.98	1.23	0.60[e]
1964	1.28	0.94	1.23	0.59[e]
1965	1.14	0.92	1.25	0.77[e]
1966	1.02	0.85	1.22	0.77[e]
1967	0.92[f]	0.77	1.14	0.67[e]

SOURCE: Col. 1, U.S. Savings and Loan League. Loans delinquent two months or more. Quarterly averages are based on monthly data reported by a representative group of associations. Col. 2, Life Insurance Association of America. All city loans (not merely residential loans) delinquent two months or more, including loans in foreclosure, as reported by companies accounting for about 80 per cent of total assets of all United States insurance companies. Col. 3, Mortgage Bankers Association of America. Residential mortgage loans on one- to four-family units delinquent two months or more, including loans in foreclosure. Col. 4, National Association of Mutual Savings Banks. Loans delinquent three months or more. Loans in foreclosure are included beginning in 1956. Through March 1958, estimated from separate rates reported for FHA-insured, VA-guaranteed, and conventional loans.

[a] Average of quarterly rate.

[b] Average of second, third and fourth quarters.

[c] Average of third and fourth quarters.

[d] Excluding loans in process of foreclosure.

[e] Not comparable with 1959 and earlier years because of increase in coverage of the survey and the change in classification of loans from total mortgages to one- to four-family housing loans.

[f] Average of first three quarters.

n.a. = not available.

closely compared, since they reflect in part differing definitions of delinquency and lender practices among the lender groups. The significant
thing is the broadly similar temporal movements shown in the several
series.

Delinquency, like foreclosure, was very low through the early and
middle 1950's. But it began to rise in the recession of 1957–58, well
before foreclosure rates began to rise much. The rise continued through
1961 for all four types of lender. Thereafter delinquency rates flattened
out for savings and loan associations and mutual savings banks, although
they continued to rise for life insurance companies and mortgage bankers. Sensitivity to periods of recession is evident in all four series. In
general, 1963 was about the peak year of delinquency experience for all
lender groups except mutual savings banks. For all four types 1967
brought a fairly sharp decline in delinquency.

The delinquency data collected by the Mortgage Bankers Association are particularly valuable because they permit comparison among
FHA, VA, conventional loans and of what may be called "casual" with
serious delinquency. The quarterly rates reported by the MBA for each
of the three types of loans, and for one, two, and three months or more
delinquency, are shown on Table 11 and Chart 8.

The rising delinquency of the late 1950's and early 1960's affected
all three types of mortgage, the least affected being conventional loans
and the most FHA loans. The conventional loan series are by far the
most stable, both over the entire period and cyclically.

An even more interesting feature of Chart 8 is the comparative behavior of "casual" (one month) and more serious delinquency. One-
month arrearage in mortgage payments rose little over the entire twelve-
year period, showing mainly a seasonal pattern, with peaks at the year
ends. This seasonal pattern is especially prominent for conventional
loans. One-month delinquency might almost be said to have shown
characteristic norms, at slightly below 1.5 per cent for conventional loans
and somewhat higher for FHA's and VA's. The one-month delinquency
rate for conventional home mortgages was lower in 1966–67 than in the
mid-1950's.

The clearest feature of the chart is the much greater rise in more
serious delinquency through 1963–64. Two-month delinquency rates
climbed more than one-month rates, and those for three months rose
most sharply of all. This was true for each of the three types of loan.
It is also significant that, although casual delinquency showed little cycle
sensitivity, serious delinquency showed clear cyclical swings in each of
the recessions of 1953–54, 1957–58, and 1960–61. This is evident in

TABLE 11

Mortgage Bankers Association, Nonfarm Residential Mortgage Delinquency, by Degree of Delinquency and Type of Loan, 1953-68

(percentage of number of given type of loan held)

Year	FHA-Insured Loans Delinquent: One Month (1)	Two Months (2)	Three Months or More (3)	VA-Guaranteed Loans Delinquent: One Month (4)	Two Months (5)	Three Months or More (6)	Conventional Loans Delinquent: One Month (7)	Two Months (8)	Three Months or More (9)	All Loans Delinquent: One Month (10)	Two Months (11)	Three Months or More (12)
1953	1.82	.30	.12	2.36	.44	.20	1.54	.32	.18	1.93	.35	.16
1954	1.76	.31	.17	2.17	.45	.22	1.26	.31	.18	1.79	.36	.19
1955	1.61	.26	.13	1.95	.37	.19	1.14	.25	.14	1.64	.30	.16
1956	1.62	.26	.13	2.04	.40	.22	1.20	.27	.15	1.72	.32	.17
1957	1.49	.24	.11	1.92	.37	.25	1.07	.25	.14	1.60	.30	.18
1958	1.46	.30	.14	2.09	.46	.32	1.06	.26	.16	1.66	.36	.22
1959	1.46	.28	.18	2.01	.44	.32	1.07	.26	.17	1.61	.35	.24
1960	1.64	.35	.28	2.14	.47	.37	1.09	.27	.19	1.73	.38	.30
1961	1.98	.46	.52	2.41	.56	.58	1.21	.30	.24	2.00	.46	.49
1962	2.13	.48	.72	2.38	.54	.64	1.33	.26	.22	2.08	.46	.59
1963	2.36	.60	.82	2.58	.62	.73	1.35	.30	.26	2.26	.56	.68
1964	2.32	.58	.84	2.43	.58	.74	1.32	.28	.25	2.18	.53	.70
1965	2.42	.60	.85	2.45	.58	.74	1.31	.30	.28	2.24	.54	.71
1966	2.49	.58	.83	2.44	.56	.69	1.34	.30	.30	2.27	.52	.69
1967	2.59	.58	.74	2.44	.54	.61	1.40	.30	.30	2.33	.52	.62
1968[a]	2.46	.53	.62	2.24	.47	.49	1.32	.28	.23	2.19	.47	.51

both Charts 7 and 8. Although there is evidence that the declining mortgage performance between the mid-1950's and the early 1960's was more structural than cyclical in origin, the data do show clearly that income and employment changes reflect themselves fairly promptly in home mortgage delinquency performance.[6] It was this combination of evidence that gave rise, in the early 1960's, to growing concern regarding home mortgage quality and motivated this and other studies of the problem.

5. Other Delinquency and Foreclosure Studies

In response to the rising incidence of mortgage loan difficulties, the Veterans' Administration, the Federal Housing Administration and the Housing and Home Finance Agency all made special studies of defaulted or foreclosed loans in 1961 and 1962. In addition, the United States Savings and Loan League, using some of the same data we employed, reported their own findings with respect to the causes of delinquency. Their results are summarized in the USSLL Occasional Paper No. 2, *Anatomy of the Residential Mortgage.* The major conclusions are briefly

[6] An effort was made earlier to test the sensitivity of mortgage delinquency to movements of employment and income by correlating quarterly levels and changes in delinquency in the twelve MBA reporting regions with the relative movements of income and employment in those regions over the years 1954–60. None of the correlations were significant. (See NBER, *44th Annual Report,* New York, 1964, pp. 121–124.) There are probably two reasons for this. First, the period was one in which structural changes in housing markets were more pronounced than cycles in employment. Second, it is known that mortgage performance problems are more closely associated with metropolitan areas than with broad regional areas. Separate delinquency data for metropolitan areas are not readily available, although some large mortgage lenders have made metropolitan area studies for their own guidance. Region of the country was one of the variables in our regression equations in analyzing the sample data, but only cross-section performance data were secured. Hence no analysis of differential performance movements among regions could be made.

Notes to Table 11

SOURCE: Calculated from *National Delinquency Survey,* compiled by the Mortgage Bankers Association of America from reports on member holdings of residential loans of one- to four-family units. Loans in foreclosure are included with loans delinquent three months or more. Annual estimates are arithmetic means of the reported quarterly rates. The entry for 1953 covers only the third and fourth quarters.

[a] Average of first three quarters.

CHART 8

Home Mortgage Delinquency, by Degree of Delinquency and Type of Loan, 1953–68

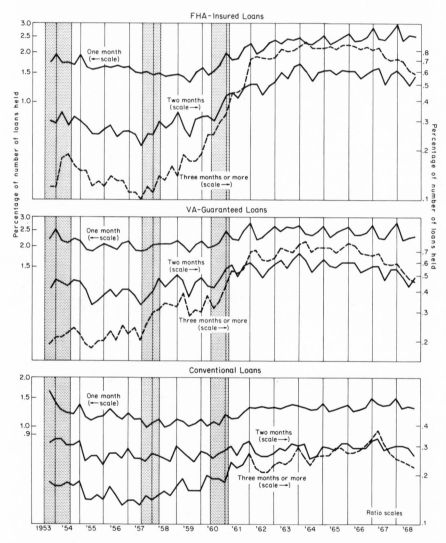

SOURCE: Quarterly data reported by Mortgage Bankers Association. See source for Table 11.

NOTE: Shaded areas represent business cycle contractions; unshaded areas, expansions (monthly chronology).

summarized here. Those interested in more detail should consult the original studies.

THE VETERANS' ADMINISTRATION STUDY [7]

This study, published in April 1962, covered all VA-guaranteed loans which were in default as of December 31, 1960, plus all new defaults reported during the four-month period January 1 to April 30, 1961.[8]

The following patterns emerged from the analysis of the reported claims. (1) Loans made to Korean war veterans showed a higher rate of claims than loans made to veterans of World War II. (2) Younger borrowers, particularly those under 30 years of age, showed a higher incidence of claims than their older counterparts.[9] (3) The incidence of claims was found to decrease sharply with the increases in borrowers' equity, so that, as one might expect, the chance of default resulting in a claim decreased as the age of the loan increased. The most dangerous period appeared to be the first three years, but the incidence of claims remained fairly high up to seven years. (4) Claims appeared to be directly related to longer initial term-to-maturity and higher loan-to-value ratio. (5) On the other hand, "no no-down-payment loans" (loans which covered the full selling price of the property plus loan closing costs) showed a somewhat lower incidence of claims than simple no-down-payment loans in which the loan simply covered the full purchase price. The probable explanation for this anomaly is that the "no no-down-payment loans" were "seasoned," since this type of loan had been unavailable for several years. (6) The purchase price of the home was found positively related to the percentage of defaults resulting in claims up to $15,000, but beyond that level the relationship was negative. Since neither time nor loan-to-value ratios were held constant, however,

[7] Veterans' Administration, *Report of Loan Service and Claims Study*, Washington, D.C., April 1962.

[8] VA regulations require that holders of VA-guaranteed mortgages notify the VA within 105 days of the date of any default. Furthermore, the lender may file a claim with the VA whenever at least three monthly instalments are in arrears. Reported defaults may be "cured" before or after claims are made, and foreclosure may or may not follow the making of claims. VA defaults were somewhat below their record level when the study was made, but claims and foreclosures were the highest ever recorded for the VA program. This suggests that "casual" delinquency was a smaller percentage of total delinquency when the study was made than had previously been the case.

[9] It is noteworthy that the claims pattern differed from the default pattern with respect to age. While fewer defaults took place in the under-30 age group than in the 30–39 group (10 per cent vs. 55 per cent of the total), 24 per cent of the defaults in the under-30 group resulted in claims, whereas only 14 per cent of the 30–39 group failed to cure their default.

it is difficult to draw any firm conclusions from this finding. (7) In those cases where the lender and the borrower agreed on the primary reason for default of the loan, "curtailment of income" was the most frequently cited (39 per cent of all cases). Among lenders, "improper regard for obligations" was very frequently cited as the primary cause (26 per cent of the cases). Of the remaining reasons for default, death or illness (16 per cent) was the only one that was cited as important in more than a few cases.

THE FEDERAL HOUSING ADMINISTRATION STUDY [10]

The FHA study was based on several types of analyses: (1) an underwriting reprocessing of a 20 per cent sample of single-family homes acquired by the FHA through foreclosure between July 1, 1961, and March 31, 1962; (2) an analysis of new credit reports on borrowers, made at the time of foreclosure, for essentially this same sample; (3) a comparison of the underwriting ratings and transaction characteristics of acquired properties with the ratings and characteristics of all mortgages insured in 1958–61 or in the calendar year 1954; (4) several intensive studies of the experience of particular insuring offices; and (5) an examination of the operating statistics normally maintained by the agency.

Analysis of the cross classifications and frequency distributions revealed the following noteworthy relationships: (1) The age of the loan appeared to be an important factor in determining whether or not foreclosure would occur. As with VA loans, FHA mortgages which had been insured in the three years immediately preceding the study accounted for the greatest proportion of acquisition. (2) Lower-priced homes had a higher acquisition ratio than homes in the higher price brackets. (This was found to be true even when loan-to-value ratios were held constant.) (3) Low down payment mortgages showed a much higher acquisition rate than mortgages with higher down payments. (4) Longer-term mortgages showed higher acquisition ratios than shorter-term, even when corrections were made for differences in property values. (5) Borrower characteristics, as measured by the FHA rating system, were considerably more important than property and location characteristics in contributing to mortgage mortality.

With regard to the FHA's risk rating system,[11] it was found that

[10] Federal Housing Administration, *FHA Experience with Mortgage Foreclosures and Property Acquisitions,* Washington, D.C., January 1963.

[11] Until 1964 all loans offered for FHA insurance were subjected to an underwriting "risk rating" based on a combination of mortgage, property and bor-

(1) composite underwriting ratings below 60 resulted in three and one-half times as many acquisitions as ratings of 60 and above. In addition, comparison of new risk ratings made at the time of foreclosure with those made at the time of insurance revealed that (2) property ratings at foreclosure were considerably lower than those which had been assigned at the time of insurance, and (3) initial borrower ratings for acquired properties were generally very low. Furthermore, (4) comparison of new credit reports made as of the time of foreclosure with original credit reports indicated that 29 per cent of the foreclosure cases would have been rejected if the original credit report had been accurate and complete. This last finding led the FHA Commissioner to take administrative measures designed to improve the quality of the credit reports which serve as a basis for assigning borrower ratings. The FHA risk ratings appeared to be at least a fair guide to mortgage quality if the recorded information on which the index was based was reliable, but that was frequently not the case. Subsequently, FHA dependence on numerical risk ratings was abandoned (see preceding footnote).

THE HOUSING AND HOME FINANCE AGENCY STUDY [12]

This study was based on a survey of mortgage foreclosures on single-family homes in six metropolitan areas—Chicago, Dallas, Detroit, Los Angeles, New York, and Philadelphia—from April 1, 1961, through March 31, 1962. Data were obtained on 2,442 cases—519 FHA, 853 VA, and 1,070 conventional loans. Several sources of information were used, including case docket files of the FHA, VA, or lending institutions, and mail questionnaires and interviews with foreclosed borrowers.

Although there were some differences among the six areas and types of mortgages, it is possible to make these generalizations from the frequency patterns observed: (1) Lower-priced homes showed higher foreclosure rates than higher-priced homes for both VA and FHA loans, but for conventional loans foreclosures were concentrated in the highest

rower characteristics. The rating factors included the maturity of the loan relative to the estimated economic life of the residence, the loan-to-value ratio, locational and physical property characteristics, mortgage payment and housing expense relationship to estimated effective mortgagor income, and a credit rating of the borrower. To be accepted for insurance, a loan was required to have a "rating pattern" of at least 50 points out of a possible 100. Ratings from 50 to 59 were considered "marginal," although acceptable. Since 1964 no over-all rating pattern has been used and numerical ratings have been dropped altogether. Now the underwriter must rate the borrower, the property, and the location as "reject," "fair," "good," or "excellent."

[12] Housing and Home Finance Agency, *Mortgage Foreclosures in Six Metropolitan Areas,* Washington, D.C., June 1963.

and lowest price brackets, giving a U-shaped distribution.[13] (2) The number of foreclosures was positively related to loan-to-value ratios, and in those cases where comparison was possible it appeared that foreclosure rates were also higher for lower down payment loans. (3) The same kind of relationship appeared to hold for initial term to maturity, with longer-term loans showing both greater numbers and greater rates of foreclosure than shorter-term loans. (4) The age of the loan again emerged as a significant factor, with foreclosures declining sharply from the second through the seventh years. (5) Loans involving junior financing showed relatively high foreclosure. (6) Borrowers who had high housing expense-to-income ratios appeared to be especially vulnerable to foreclosure.

This last relationship, not examined in the other studies, is worth special notice. Of the foreclosed loans, 33 per cent of the FHA and 41 per cent of the VA had housing expense-to-income ratios of 30 per cent or more. In most of the areas studied, the percentages for conventional loans were fairly similar. Although exact comparison is impossible, the adverse influence at high expense-to-income ratios is strongly suggested. As the data presented above show, the average ratio of housing expense to income for section 203 FHA loans as a whole never exceeded 22 per cent in any year between 1940 and 1960. For VA prior-approval loans, the average ratio never exceeded 23 per cent on new loans guaranteed in any year from 1954 to 1960. Clearly the housing expense-to-income ratio was unusually high on a disproportionate share of the foreclosed loans.[14]

Questions dealing with the reasons for foreclosure revealed expected differences between borrowers' and lenders' views of what caused the trouble. Both cited "curtailment of income" as the reason in the greatest number of cases; but whereas lenders deemed "improper regard for obligations" and "excessive obligations" to be next in order of importance, borrowers so listed "death or illness" and "marital difficulties." "Marital difficulties" did rank well up among lenders' reasons as well. Borrowers would not be likely to view themselves as having an improper regard for obligations. It is probably significant that borrowers cited

13 This latter finding must be interpreted with caution, however, since what was measured was the absolute number of foreclosures rather than rates. It is quite likely that this apparently different pattern mainly reflects the price distribution of homes on which conventional loans were made.

14 This finding, it should be noted, is at variance with our own study which found payment-to-income ratios unrelated to either delinquency or foreclosure risk.

"excessive obligations" as a problem only half as frequently as lenders, and that they cited "death or illness" twice as frequently.

THE UNITED STATES SAVINGS AND LOAN LEAGUE STUDY [15]

Since the sampling procedures the League employed will be described in detail in subsequent sections and in Appendix A, we merely point out that the study was national in scope and included over 6,500 conventional loans, roughly half of which were in good standing. The study made no attempt to investigate the causes of foreclosure, but centered its attention on (1) loan, property and borrower characteristics in general, and (2) the difference in these characteristics for current loans vis-a-vis delinquent loans. No significance testing was performed, nor was there any systematic attempt to remove the influence of variables other than the one being studied. The technique was merely to run cross tabulations on the two groups of loans, showing what percentage of the currents and what percentage of the delinquents had a given characteristic.

Loan Characteristics. Most delinquencies were found to have occurred between the second and fifth year of the loan's life. It should be noted however, that the age distribution of delinquent loans did not differ drastically from that for current loans. Thus while 65 per cent of the delinquent loans had been on the books between two and five years, 53 per cent of the current loans were so classified. Furthermore, if all loans under seven years of age are singled out, 87 per cent of the delinquents and 83 per cent of the currents are included. Term to maturity did not appear to differ much between current and delinquent loans, but loan-to-value ratio did. Generally speaking, loans with high ratios appeared to be more prone to delinquency. With regard to loan purpose, refinancing appeared to be a source of trouble. While refinancing was listed as the purpose of only 17 per cent of the current loans, 29 per cent of the delinquents fell into this category. The study also found that "a large portion of the delinquent loans came from those loans with higher interest rates." It is possible to argue (as the author of the study did) that loan officers apparently demand higher rates from marginal borrowers to compensate for the higher risks. In view of the rather large movements in interest rates over the postwar period, however, it is virtually impossible to separate the inter-temporal variability from the cross-sectional. Junior financing was found to be asso-

[15] United States Savings and Loan League, *Anatomy of the Residential Mortgage*, Chicago, 1964.

ciated with greater delinquency risk, only 17 per cent of the current loans but 29 per cent of the delinquents reporting that junior financing had been employed. Note that these percentages are identical to the ones cited above concerning refinancing.

Property Characteristics. Location (in city, new suburb, built-up suburb) did not appear to be an important factor except where the loan was made to a builder. Builder loans in new suburbs appeared to carry higher risks of delinquency. The age of the home did not provide any insights, but purchase price did. Generally speaking, properties in the $10,000–$15,000 price bracket produced the greatest delinquency problem.

Borrower Characteristics. Income distributions for current and delinquent borrowers were similar, but delinquency was relatively more frequent among those whose source of income was their own business and among borrowers who moonlighted. Self-employed persons, unskilled laborers and salesmen were found to represent the greatest risks of deliquency, while executives, white-collar workers and professionals represented the lowest. Widowed and divorced borrowers tended to a somewhat less favorable delinquency experience, and there appeared to be a positive relationship between number of dependents and the incidence of delinquency. Younger borrowers (those under 40) showed a definite tendency toward higher delinquency, and beyond 40 the risk of delinquency was found to decrease with age. Finally, borrowers who had held their main job for less than five years were judged to be relatively poor risks.

Miscellaneous Points. In listing reasons for the delinquency, improper regard for obligations, loss of income, excessive obligations and death or illness were the more frequently cited, in that order. The first two reasons alone accounted for more than 60 per cent of the cases where a reason was given. Perhaps not unexpectedly, almost half (44 per cent) of the delinquent loans had been in trouble repeatedly and another 35 per cent had had intermittent difficulties. It is also noteworthy that nearly two out of three delinquent loans still had more than 90 per cent of the original balance owing.

WEAKNESSES OF THE STUDIES

None of these studies provided very solid ground on which to base conclusions relative to mortgage quality. In the first place, the government studies concentrated on only one type of performance evidence-foreclosure. No attempt was made to analyze delinquent versus current loans to see what factors are associated with delinquency. Nor was there any effort (except some slight analysis in the VA study) to determine why some delinquencies result in foreclosure while others do not. The U.S. Savings and Loan League study, on the other hand, looked at the causes of delinquency, but ignored foreclosure altogether.

Second, the findings are difficult to compare and evaluate in moving from one study to another. The VA study, for example, related various property, borrower and loan characteristics to "incidence of claims," i.e., the percentage of defaulted loans which resulted in the filing of a claim. The FHA study compared property, borrower and loan characteristics of properties acquired in 1961 and insured in 1958–61 with the population of all loans insured in that same period, in the form of frequency distributions showing what percentage of all loans insured fell into each of several classes. The weakest data by far were those in the HHFA report. Except for some general allusions to the characteristics of mortgages made in the period preceding the study, the analysis was confined almost exclusively to simple frequency distributions of the characteristics of the loans foreclosed. Whether the distributions represented anything other than the distribution of all loans, good and bad, it would be impossible to say from the study.

Beyond these weaknesses in the design of the cross-tabulation schemes, the studies also suffered from other shortcomings. (1) No significance testing was performed, and thus no basis exists for determining whether the relationships observed have any real meaning or whether they largely reflect random variation. (2) The samples on which the government studies were based left much to be desired. Only the HHFA study gave any attention at all to conventional loans, and in that case the "sample" is little more than a collection of foreclosed loans. Since no over-all delinquency or forecloseure data were available for the six metropolitan areas sampled, it is impossible to determine the universe which the sample is supposed to represent. The U.S. Savings and Loan League study provided adequate coverage of the conventional sector (FHA and VA loans were excluded) but it contained no information whatsoever on foreclosure. (3) The number and definitions of variables studied differed considerably among the studies, making comparisons hazardous at best.

Because of these weaknesses and limitations the studies did little more than suggest tentative hypotheses for further testing. These hypotheses are:

1. Delinquency and foreclosure rates vary directly with:
   a. Loan-to-value ratio
   b. Contract interest rate
   c. Housing expense-to-income ratio
   d. Number of dependents
2. Foreclosure (but not delinquency) rates tend to vary directly with term to maturity.
3. Delinquency and foreclosure rates tend to vary inversely with:
   a. Age of loan
   b. Borrower's equity
   c. Purchase price of property
   d. Age of borrower
   e. Borrower's occupational skill level
4. Loans involving junior financing or refinancing are more likely to lead to delinquency and foreclosure than loans on which no junior financing is present or loans which are made for some purpose other than to replace an existing mortgage.

6. The Present Study

RESEARCH STRATEGY

Our own study, formulated in the light of these earlier investigations, attempts to remedy their major shortcomings. In the first place, we study loan delinquency as well as foreclosure. Second, we use sample data not only for "bad" loans (those delinquent or in foreclosure) but also for "good" ones. By comparing the characteristics of paired classes (current vs. noncurrent, current vs. foreclosures, and delinquent vs. foreclosures), we can estimate statistically the contribution of each characteristic to delinquency and foreclosure. Third, we cover conventional as well as FHA and VA loans. Fourth, we study the loans made by each of three major types of mortgage lenders. Fifth, the sample is nationwide in coverage. We would have liked to work with only terminated loans in order to be able to clearly identify those which were genuinely "bad" or "good." As it is, we classified a loan as good if it was not in difficulty at the time of sampling and bad if it was in trouble. In addition, we would have preferred to have had samples taken at a number of different points in time. We found, however, that neither of these procedures was possible.

Our data were collected by the United States Savings and Loan League (USSLL), the Mortgage Bankers Association (MBA), and the National Association of Mutual Savings Banks (NAMSB). These organizations conducted surveys at various dates in 1963. They attempted to secure reliable samples of both current and noncurrent (delinquent and foreclosed) loans of representative classes of their membership.[16]

The USSLL survey provided data covering 4,902 current and 1,570 noncurrent (ninety or more days delinquent or in foreclosure) conventional home loans from thirty-eight representative member associations. The MBA survey secured data from 36 mutual savings banks, 41 commercial banks, and 105 mortgage companies from their regular reporters for the association's quarterly surveys. Seventy-three savings banks participated in the NAMSB survey. Their data were added to those collected from the 36 mutual savings banks in the MBA survey, making 109 savings banks in all. In toto, the characteristics of 12,581 one- to four-family home mortgages were secured, 7,979 of them current and 4,602 noncurrent. Of these latter, 3,254 were ninety days or more delinquent, and another 1,348 in process of foreclosure. In the combined samples, 7,373 loans were conventionals, 2,700 were FHA's, and 2,508 were VA's.

An effort was made to include in each survey those characteristics that operating experience and earlier studies had indicated might be of special importance to mortgage quality. Loan and borrower characteristics were given greater stress than property characteristics, partly because earlier studies had indicated their greater importance and partly because the records used provided little meaningful property characteristics.

It was hoped that each survey could provide the same variables and on a comparable basis, but this was only partly successful. All three surveys did, however, provide the following information: the three presumptively important terms—(1) loan-to-value ratio, (2) initial term to maturity, and (3) mortgage payment-to-income ratio—(4) borrower income itself, (5) occupation, (6) marital status, (7) number of dependents, (8) age, and (9) the region in which the loan originated. Only the USSLL data, which fortunately were the major source of information on conventional loans, provided two other important types of information: (10) the purpose of the loan (i.e., whether for home construction or repair, home purchase or refinancing), and (11) whether there was junior financing involved in the transaction.

The Analysis

Given the large number of observations and the substantial number of characteristics included in the data, multiple regression analysis

[16] For technical description of the sampling methods and copies of the forms employed, see Appendix A.

appeared to offer the best framework for the study. The advantage of multiple regression over most other techniques is that it permits the isolation and holding constant of the effect of *all* variables included in the analysis, and provides measures of the relative influence of these variables upon the phenomena being investigated. Simpler methods do not permit this, so that if, as is almost always the case, variables operate jointly to produce a given effect, the results can be very misleading. Still more sophisticated techniques, such as multiple linear and non-linear discriminant functions, were explored but found impracticable. Multiple regression was supplemented by Lorenz-type tests of the "risk indexes" developed from the regressions. The purpose of these tests was to ascertain whether the functions had more discriminating power than was indicated in the usual tests of statistical significance.[17]

These analyses provided the key "cross-sectional" findings of the study. However, we attempted to apply the cross-sectional results to the question whether there had been, on balance, an improvement or deterioration in the quality of home mortgages over the postwar years. The manner in which this was done is described in Chapter III, which also summarizes our findings with regard to changes in quality over time. The major cross-sectional results of the regression analysis are presented in the next chapter. Technical detail is kept to a minimum in the text. More technical treatment of results is included in Appendix B.

[17] For more complete discussion of the computational techniques employed, see Appendix B.

II

The Major Determinants of Differential
Mortgage Quality

In order to assess the influence of various combinations of loan, borrower and property characteristics on mortgage quality, we found it desirable to break down the data in a number of ways. The first division was made according to loan status—loans being classified as current (no payment arrearages or arrearages of less than ninety days), delinquent (ninety days or more), and in foreclosure. Using loan status as the dependent variable, we then ran regressions for current vs. noncurrent (delinquents and loans in foreclosure), delinquent vs. loans in foreclosure, and, for the USSLL data, current vs. loans in foreclosure.[1] Second, we ran separate sets of regressions for each subsample, USSLL, MBA, and NAMSB. The purpose here was twofold. Given the large number of observations and variables, it was more convenient computationally to work on the subsamples separately. In addition, there were important differences among the subsamples which would have been "washed out" had they been combined. A further division of the regressions was made according to the number and definition of variables in each of the subsamples. In the so-called individual versions of the equations we made maximum use of the information available to us. In the "pooled" versions, however, we included only variables on which we had data in each of the subsamples, and these variables were defined in

---

[1] It was necessary to restrict our comparisons to paired cases, since the regression framework will not accommodate a dummy dependent variable which assumes more than two values. Multiple discriminant analysis offers a possible alternative, but, given the large number of variables and observations we had to work with, it proved to be much too cumbersome from a computational standpoint.

such a way that we had compatability among the equations. This permitted us to focus attention on similarities and differences among the three subsamples. The end result of all this was a set of thirteen regression equations. Full detail on these equations, along with relevant statistical tests, is provided in Appendix B.[2] The sections which follow, however, are intended to set forth and evaluate the findings without going into unnecessary technical detail.

1. Delinquency Risk

Delinquency risk equations were developed by treating the dependent variable, loan status, as a dummy. Thus the variable was assigned a value of zero if the loan was not currently in difficulty (current) and a value of one if it was either ninety or more days delinquent or in foreclosure (noncurrent). While we refer to such functions as risk index equations, they have often been referred to in econometric studies as linear probability functions. Ostensibly the function is linear because it employs the technique of multiple linear regression. It is considered a probability function because it is estimated by using a dependent variable which can assume a value of zero or one. Thus the output of the estimated equation, when particular values are assigned to the dependent variables, should be a number between zero and one. The closer the value falls to one (noncurrent in our classification scheme), the greater the *probability* that the loan will be delinquent. The closer the value falls to zero, the less the probability of delinquency. Unfortunately, there is no way of guaranteeing that a particular combination of observed values of the variables will invariably lead to a solution falling between zero and one. In cases where negative values or values greater than one arise, it is not possible to assign a probability interpretation to them. We choose, therefore, to call the regression functions *risk equations* and to call the outputs of these equations *risk indexes*. It is clear that if the equations have good discriminating power, lower values for the out-

[2] The general form of the regression equations is:

$$r_d = a_1 + a_2 RLS + a_3 T + a_4 RPI + O_i + DN_i + SM_i + AB_i + P_i$$
$$+ FJ + TLD_i + TLN_i + R_i$$

The subscripted variables are used to show the presence of two or more dummy classes, and the variable names (mnemonic symbols) are as defined in the text. In the case of dummy variables it is not necessary to show both a coefficient and a variable, since whenever the variable falls within a given class it will assume the value of the coefficient and whenever it falls outside it will assume a value of zero.

put indicate low risk and high values indicate high risk, whether or not such values are less than zero or greater than one.

INDIVIDUAL EQUATIONS

As was indicated above, the individual equations for the three sets of data (USSLL, MBA, and NAMSB) use the maximum number of variables and data available in each subsample. This means that because there were differences among the questionnaires and response rates, the coefficients of the three regression equations cannot be directly compared. It has the advantage, however, of making maximum use of the information the lender had at his disposal at the time the loan was made. Since we were primarily interested in discovering the relationship between loan quality and variables which might enter into the lending decision, we did not explicitly consider such variables as the age of the loan when the sample was drawn, stated reasons for delinquency, or borrowers' status at the time of delinquency (or drawing of the sample). Variables which were included in one or more of the regressions are loan-to-value ratio (RLS), term to maturity (T), monthly payment-to-income ratio (RPI), borrower occupation (O), number of dependents (DN), marital status (SM), borrower age (AB), loan purpose (P), junior financing (FJ), type of lender (TLD), type of loan (TLN), and region (R). While data were available on age and location of property, preliminary analysis did not lead us to believe such variables would be important. The same may be said for property value and borrower income. Simple cross tabulations relating these variables to loan status failed to reveal any relationship. It was expected that two of the variables listed above, loan-to-value ratio and payment-to-income ratio, would capture the important value and income relationships since they link them to the pertinent loan characteristics, the former giving a measure of the borrower's vested interest and the latter his financial burden. Given the large number of variables we had to work with some economizing was essential for computation purposes.

The discriminating power of the equations themselves was tested in three ways—through over-all F ratios, analysis of coefficients of determination (R^2's), and Lorenz tests. The F ratios are used to determine whether the regressions are or are not significant. They are computed by forming the ratio "regression variance/residual variance." Since the numerator of the ratio measures how much variance is explained by the fitted regression function and residual variance measures how much is left unexplained, it follows that large ratios are indicative of good discriminating power and that small ratios raise doubts about the estimated relations. Any given ratio may, however, be due solely to chance, so it becomes necessary to determine how large a ratio pure chance might lead us to expect. F tables exist for this purpose. Thus by comparing our results with those found in an F table, we can determine whether our ratios are likely to be due to chance or whether the regressions upon which they are based are, in fact, significant.

The second statistic which was employed, the coefficient of determination, is useful for two reasons. First, it expresses the ratio of the sum of the squared deviations "captured" by the regression plane to the sum of the squared deviations around the mean of the dependent variable. Thus it shows the proportion of deviations explained by (or attributable to) the regression. A second interpretation of the statistic relates it to the coefficient of multiple correlation. More specifically, it can be shown that R^2, the coefficient of determination, can be obtained by squaring the coefficient of multiple correlation, R. These two interpretations, taken together, underscore the usefulness of the statistic. It will readily be seen that its value will range between zero and one and that the closer it lies to one, the greater is the discriminating power of the regression.

Lorenz tests, which are not part of the standard statistical repertoire, were developed to show graphically how well the regressions distinguished between "good" and "bad" loans.[3] The basic idea was to use the regression equations to calculate a risk index for each loan in the sample and to array the loans according to the size of the index, beginning with the smallest values and proceeding through the largest. At each value of the index two ratios were calculated, one showing the percentage of all loans in the sample having an index value equal to or less than the one indicated, and another showing the percentage of "bad" loans thus classified. These ratios were then plotted on graphs, such as Chart 9, below. It should be immediately apparent that a function which has low discriminating power will result in a series of plots near the reference line, a 45 degree diagonal from the origin. Conversely, high discrimination would yield plots near the horizontal and vertical axes. Thus the closer the Lorenz curve lies to the axes (the more bow it has), the greater the degree of discrimination.

[3] The authors wish to acknowledge the considerable help of Donald Steward in developing these tests. Mr. Steward, a member of the Social Science Research Institute computational staff, took some rather vague ideas, expressed them in more rigorous form, and worked out the computer programs necessary to develop the tests.

The individual versions of the equations for all three subsamples yielded F ratios which were significant at the 1 per cent level, thereby indicating that at least some discrimination was achieved.[4] The ratio was highest for the USSLL equation and lowest for the MBA. Similar patterns emerged for the coefficients of determination and the Lorenz tests. The USSLL equation produced the highest coefficient of determination (about 11.5 per cent), followed by the NAMSB version (just under 5 per cent) and the MBA (under 4 per cent). These values are quite low by any standards, but they are not totally meaningless. If it were possible to predict quality absolutely on the basis of the few variables and simple functional forms we have included, mortgage underwriters would long ago have developed rating schemes to reflect this fact. The truth is many variables interact, and in ways not yet imagined. That does not mean that studies of this type are fruitless, for in spite of what remains unexplained, valuable insights emerge. A second point to bear in mind is that cross-section microeconomic data such as we used typically yield much lower R^2's, than the time series data to which so many of us have become accustomed. This is true largely because these observations can be explained by circumstances that are idiosyncratic to individual households and have no particular relevance or interest from the point of view of economic analysis. Finally, the use of a dummy dependent variable and the large number of observations almost certainly reduced the R^2's below what they otherwise would have been. Consider the influence of dummies. If the sample on which the regression is being run is roughly 50 per cent current and 50 per cent noncurrent (as ours were), the expected value of the dependent variable over the whole sample must be one-half (.5). Theoretically, its value for any particular set of observations on the independent variables will fall somewhere between zero and one, with a probability of zero of its being either zero or one exactly. Yet when this calculated value is compared to the observed value (which *must* be either zero or one by definition) any deviation will lower the value of the R^2, sometimes by a substantial amount. In spite of these anomalies, the *relative* sizes of the coefficients are probably indicative of the differences

---

[4] The statement "significant at the 1 per cent level" means simply that when we assert some statement is true (for example, that the equations *do* discriminate between good and bad loans), we can expect to be wrong no more than one out of a hundred times. Similarly, if we were to say "significant at the 5 per cent level," we could expect to be wrong one out of every twenty times. We follow standard usage of these terms in subsequent sections by referring to 1 per cent significance as "highly significant" and 5 per cent significance as "significant." Those interested in seeing the statistics upon which our statements are based can find them in Appendix B.

CHART 9

Lorenz Curves, Current vs. Noncurrent, Individual

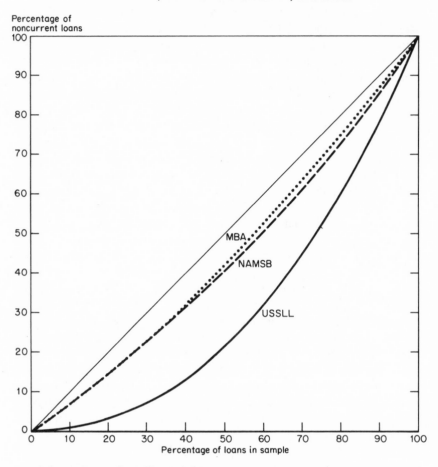

Percentage of
noncurrent loans

Percentage of loans in sample

SOURCE: Appendix Tables B14–B16.

in the discriminating power among the equations, and for this reason, together with its familiarity, we will continue to use the statistic.

The Lorenz curves in Chart 9 confirm the findings of the R^2 tests as to the relative discriminating power of the three equations.[5] It is obvi-

---

[5] The curves referred to do not, strictly speaking, fall under the usual definition of a Lorenz curve. The manner in which an ordinary Lorenz curve is constructed insures that it will increase at a constant or increasing rate throughout its length. The method we used for plotting values provided no such assurance. Nevertheless a freehand fitting of curves to the plotted values yielded, perhaps

ous from this chart, however, that the equations do a better job of discriminating between good and bad loans than the low value of the R^2's might suggest. Indeed, the rather pronounced bow in the USSLL curve indicates that that equation does a fairly decent job of quality rating. This is not to suggest that the equation could not be improved upon or that misassignments occur only occasionally, but at least it indicates a step in the right direction.

With regard to the independent variables used in the regressions, a number of noteworthy points emerged.[6] We discuss these in the variables' order of appearance in the equations. Loan-to-value ratio bore a strong positive relation to delinquency risk in all three equations. In fact, it turned out to be the most important variable in both the MBA and NAMSB equations. In the USSLL equation it trailed only loan purpose and junior financing in order of importance.[7] Neither of the latter two variables appeared in the MBA and NAMSB versions. It should also be noted that the coefficient for this variable was significant at the 1 per cent level in all three equations.

The behavior of the term to maturity variable was most surprising. It differed significantly from zero only in the NAMSB equation, but it carried a negative sign in all three versions. This would seem to indicate that longer maturities are associated with a lower rather than a higher risk of delinquency. In view of the fact that most lenders (and we ourselves) regard a liberalization of terms, *ceteris paribus,* as adding to risk, how can such a phenomenon be explained? First of all, the reader must bear in mind that we are speaking only of risks of delinquency—not foreclosure or potential loss on the loan. Secondly, the negative sign might well be no more than a statistical aberration which stems from the form of the equations we employed. Of the three equations we estimated, the NAMSB version (the one in which the negative sign was significant) contained the fewest number of variables. It is worth noting in this connection that the coefficient was smallest

accidentally, curves with Lorenz characteristics. A more important reason for adopting the terminology, however, is that the curves we have constructed and Lorenz curves are designed for the same purpose—to graphically portray inequality in one distribution with reference to another.

[6] Simple correlations between the independent variables suggest that multicollinearity was not a serious problem. In all cases but one (loan-to-value ratio vs. term to maturity) the correlations were well below .2. Even in the exceptional case, the coefficient typically was below .5.

[7] Importance was measured in two ways, through partial correlation coefficients and beta coefficients. The former are self-explanatory; the latter are used to determine how many standard deviations of change occur in the dependent variable for each standard deviation change in the independent.

in the USSLL version and this is the only one in which we were able to include loan purpose and junior financing. It would appear then, that the dropping of variables, particularly loan purpose and junior financing, biases the coefficient in the negative direction. Why might this be? If, as is likely to be the case, loans for refinancing or repair or which have junior financing associated with them have shorter maturities, the latter variable could be acting as a proxy for the other two. That such a possibility is indeed likely will be seen when the pooled versions of the equations are examined. When loan purpose and junior financing were dropped from the USSLL equation, the negative coefficient grew in size and its "t" value became significant at the 1 per cent level. Furthermore, examination of scaled down (intermediate) versions of all three equations reveals that as more variables are dropped, the negative value of the coefficient increases, as does its "t" value.

Even in the most complete version of the equation (USSLL) we may not have been able to include all the relevant variables. For example, we were unable to include either wealth or liquid assets, both measures of financial strength and borrowers' ability to pay. It stands to reason that loans with shorter maturities will carry higher monthly payments. If, therefore, no explicit account is taken of financial strength and if shorter maturities are associated with weaker borrowers, results similar to ours could be expected. Shorter maturities might well be associated with weaker borrowers if lenders, in perceiving the greater (but still acceptable) risks, require a more rapid repayment of the loan to ensure a quicker buildup of equity.

In sum, it would appear that the negative signs we observed are not likely to be indicative of the "true" relationship between risk and term to maturity. Rather, it would appear that the most likely association is one of no net influence when the equation is properly specified. Even this conclusion must be interpreted with caution, however, for it applies only to what one is likely to observe in practice. If lenders were to throw all caution to the winds and require little or no buildup of equity on a property which is declining in value, defaults would almost certainly ensue.

The behavior of the monthly payment-to-income variable was hardly less surprising than that of term to maturity. It too carried a negative sign, even though it failed the significance test at the 1 per cent level. In one case, however (the MBA version), it turned out to be significant at the 5 per cent level. We had anticipated that this ratio would serve as a good measure of financial burden and would thus vary directly with delinquency risk. That it did not might be evidence that lenders have been successful in controlling this aspect of risk. Since our sample included only those loans which passed the lenders' (and in the case of FHA and VA, the underwriters') screening process, loans with dangerously high ratios may have already been filtered out. If that is the case, we may have observed only random variability in the ratio rather than variability which would be indicative of risk. This possibility seems to be borne out by some cross tabulations which we ran on the data. In the USSLL and MBA subsamples, for example, more than 96 per cent of the loans had payment-to-income ratios under 25 per cent.[8] In the NAMSB sample, 92 per cent of the loans were so classified. These figures would indicate that, for the most part, lenders imposed a fairly strict upper limit of about 25 per cent on the ratio. It could be that such a limit is well within the "safe" range and the observed delinquencies must, therefore, be attributed to other causes.

Occupation provided a good example of the need for common definitions among the samples. There is little doubt that the variable is important, but differences in occupational groupings made comparison extremely difficult. Nevertheless, a few clear-cut patterns did emerge. Salesmen showed high risk coefficients in all three equations, even though in one case (MBA) the difference between this coefficient and that of the reference group (skilled laborers) was not significant. Self-employed persons were also high risk in the one sample in which they appeared (USSLL). At the other end of the spectrum, professionals (not significant in NAMSB) and managers, executives, and proprietors (not significant in NAMSB) yielded the lowest risk coefficients.[9] The remaining occupational groups, including skilled and unskilled labor, service workers, clerical or civil service employees, and craftsmen or foremen were pretty well clustered together between the low and the high risk extremes. The one exception to this was in the USSLL sample, where white-collar workers were at the low risk end of the spectrum.

Number of dependents bore a direct relationship to risk in the USSLL version, with risk coefficients increasing steadily from the second

[8] It is perhaps worth noting that variability below the 25 per cent level was much greater for the USSLL than for the other two groups. For example, only 7 per cent of the MBA loans had ratios under 10 per cent, while 33 per cent of the USSLL loans were under this figure.

[9] The practice which both the MBA and NAMSB adopted of lumping proprietors in with managers almost certainly gave a coefficient closer to zero than would have otherwise been the case. It is clear from examining the USSLL data that self-employed persons (which includes proprietors) are high risk, while executives or managers are low.

through the eighth dependent. In the MBA and NAMSB samples, however, the variable did not turn out to be significant. Some tendency toward a direct relationship was evident, but it was far from clear-cut. In view of the fact that the USSLL equation showed the greatest discriminating power, we are inclined to accept the evidence that a direct relationship between number of dependents and risk does exist. There is also a fairly strong a priori basis for this conclusion, since larger families mean higher expenses in expenditure areas where we lacked data.

Marital status did not appear to be a significant factor in any of the equations, though the risk coefficients were uniformly lower for married than for single borrowers. In the USSLL sample, where a finer breakdown was provided, the ranking in terms of the size of the coefficients was widowed, divorced, single, and married, in that order. Borrower age was a significant factor in both the USSLL and MBA equations, but the pattern was so mixed that any conclusion must be highly tentative. Granting the exceptions, it appeared that younger borrowers (those under 40) might offer greater risks than those 40 and above. We hasten to add, however, that the evidence is far from conclusive on this point.

Loan purpose, which was included in only the USSLL sample, proved to be an extremely important determinant of risk. As one might expect, loans extended for house purchase showed the best performance, and by a considerable margin. Construction loans came next in order of risk, followed by loans for repair and, finally, refinancing. The degree of risk associated with refinancing is underscored by the fact that it carried a larger coefficient (and higher "t" value) than any other dummy variable in the equation. Junior financing, which also was excluded from the MBA and NAMSB samples, was virtually on a par with loan purpose in order of importance. Loans for which some form of secondary financing was present carried much higher risk coefficients than those without.

Region was included in the equations only to isolate the effects of geographical influence and, as one might expect, risk bore a direct relationship to regional delinquency patterns. The fact that there were significant differences among the regions indicates that failure to include the variable would have seriously biased the results. This applies particularly to the USSLL equation, where the greatest differences emerged.

None of the coefficients for lender type was significant, even though some weak patterns were in evidence.[10] Perhaps not surprisingly, loans from commercial banks and trusteed funds appeared to be somewhat less risky than loans held by mortgage bankers for their own account or for individuals. The differences were not sharp, but they may indicate that some loans in the mortgage bankers' portfolios are there because they were not salable to other institutions. Another possibility is that they reflect loans transferred back to the mortgage banker for foreclosure.

Loan type (FHA, VA, or conventional) entered into both the NAMSB and MBA equations, but since the USSLL sample included only conventional loans, the variable does not appear in that version. Surprisingly, FHA and VA loans showed significantly lower risk coefficients than conventionals. These differences were significant at the 1 per cent level for the MBA sample and at the 5 per cent level for the NAMSB. It is possible that this finding reflects only differences in underwriting and appraisal practices—factors which we could not measure. It most certainly does *not* indicate that conventionals are more risky, per se. Indeed, when the *combined* influence of this variable and the others is considered, it is likely that FHA's and VA's are more, not less, risky than conventionals. We have already noted, for example, that high loan-to-value ratios are associated with high delinquency risk. Since FHA and VA loans are likely to involve lower downpayments than conventional loans, this factor could dominate.

POOLED EQUATIONS

The pooled versions, as was noted above, were arrived at by dropping variablés for which data were not available in all three subsamples and by redefining others so as to make them compatible. We had initially intended actually to pool all of the observations and compute one equation which we could compare with similar equations for each of the subsamples. This would have enabled us to determine whether differences among the subsamples were *statistically* significant. We can make judgments about these differences, however, by merely comparing equations for each subsample. In view of the additional programming and computer time involved in developing the statistical tests associated with the initial plan, it was decided to abandon it in favor of the less sophisticated "judgment" approach.

The over-all discriminating power of the pooled equations was, as

[10] Lender type applied only to the MBA equation since loans in the USSLL and NAMSB samples were, by definition, held by savings and loan associations and mutual savings banks.

we anticipated, somewhat less than for the individual versions. All the equations, however, continued to be significant at the 1 per cent level, as measured by their F ratios.[11] R^2's (coefficients of determination) were somewhat lower for all equations, but especially for the USSLL version, where a drop from 11.5 to 8 per cent was recorded. Even so, the relative rankings were maintained, with the USSLL showing the best discriminating power, followed by NAMSB and MBA, in that order. Similar patterns were observed in the Lorenz tests (Chart 10), although the apparent loss in discriminating power there was not as great as shown the R^2's. For example, while the R^2 value in the USSLL equation declined by nearly one-third, it does not appear that the area between the reference line and the USSLL Lorenz curve diminished by more than about 20 per cent. Shifts in the MBA and NAMSB curves were negligible.

Loan-to-value ratio continued to show a strong positive relationship to risk, yielding highly significant positive coefficients in all three equations. Negative signs were again indicated for the term-to-maturity coefficients and these were significant at the 1 per cent level in both the USSLL and MBA versions, and at the 5 per cent level in the NAMSB. This tends to confirm the point made earlier, that this variable is probably serving as a proxy for some which we omitted. It will be recalled that in the individual versions only one coefficient (NAMSB) was significant. Dropping variables, as we did in the pooled versions, however, has the effect of generating larger coefficients, pushing "*t*" values over the critical level. Payment-to-income ratio once again failed to satisfy the significance tests at either the 1 per cent or 5 per cent level.

Among the occupational groupings salesmen had high risk coefficients in all three cases, although the MBA coefficient did not quite satisfy the criterion for significance. Proprietors and self-employed were among the high risks in the USSLL and NAMSB samples, but not in the MBA—possibly, as was indicated earlier, because managers were included in this group. Unskilled laborers were fairly high risk in all three cases, even though the coefficients were just at the margin of significance for the MBA and NAMSB. Service and miscellaneous workers and skilled labor were near the center of the risk spectrum, followed by clerical workers. It should be noted, however, that in the NAMSB sample, the risk coefficient was greater for clerical workers

---

[11] Actually, the F ratios for the pooled versions of the MBA and NAMSB equations were slightly higher than they were for the individual versions. This can be attributed to the fact that some variables which were not significant in the individual versions were dropped from the pooled versions.

CHART 10

Lorenz Curves, Current vs. Noncurrent, Pooled

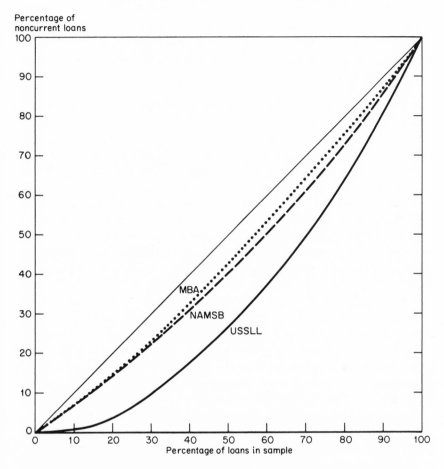

SOURCE: Appendix Tables B17–B19.

than for either skilled labor or miscellaneous. Professional and technical personnel had the lowest risk coefficient in every case, except for the USSLL, where white-collar workers (classified clerical) had the best performance. Considering the definitional problems raised by differences in the questionnaires, it was encouraging from an analytical standpoint to be able to establish the importance of occupation. One can only conclude that the nature of a borrower's employment has an important bearing on default risk, and the evidence is quite strong that there is an inverse relation between job skill and risk. The self-employed or proprietor category provides a notable, but not surprising, exception to this pattern. The fact that the risk coefficient is high for this group may be indicative of the inseparability of one's personal and business affairs. Typically, when a proprietor is facing financial problems in his business, he must resort to using his personal resources to attempt to remedy the situation.

Number of dependents proved to be significant (at the 1 per cent level) in only one equation (USSLL). Nevertheless, the same general pattern was observed here as in the individual equations. The degree of risk increased steadily with increasing numbers of dependents, except at the extremes (zero or seven or more dependents), where the results were mixed. Marital status was significant in the USSLL version, but once again failed the test in the other two. That the one coefficient which was significant showed married people to be better risks tends to confirm the earlier findings concerning this variable.

Borrower age, as in the individual versions, presented a very irregular pattern. By the greatest stretch of one's imagination, a general downward trend in risk with increasing age can be detected. Exceptions, however, occur in every sample. For the USSLL the pattern is broken by the coefficients for the 30–34 age bracket (too low) and the 50–59 bracket (too high). For the MBA the 30–34 coefficient is too high, the 35–39 too low, and the 50–59 too low. For the NAMSB the 30–34 bracket is too low and the 40–44 bracket is much too high. Considering all the exceptions, the safest course would probably be to conclude that age has no apparent systematic effect on risk.

Regional coefficients, as well as loan type and lender type, generally followed the patterns observed in the individual versions. One exception to this was under loan type in the MBA sample. In the earlier version, FHA 203 loans and other FHA's were treated separately. Lumping them together for the pooled version apparently reduced the value of the coefficient to the point where it was no longer significant.

2. Foreclosure Risk

Up to now our analysis has been concerned with only one aspect of quality—delinquency risk. We now turn our attention to a second, namely, foreclosure risk. Foreclosure risk was measured in two ways for this study: first, as a conditional probability showing risk of foreclosure, given that a loan was already in default; second, as an unconditional probability showing the risk that a current loan will end up in foreclosure. The first measure was calculated in the same way as delinquency risk, only in this case we worked exclusively with the noncurrent part of the sample, comparing loans in foreclosure with loans which were delinquent but not in foreclosure. This was done for all three subsamples and for both individual and pooled versions. The second measure was developed by comparing current loans with loans in foreclosure. Because the USSLL sample seemed to provide the best data, this second measure of foreclosure risk was developed only for that group and only in the form which made maximum use of the data available (individual).

INDIVIDUAL EQUATIONS

The discriminating power of the foreclosure risk equations proved to be somewhat better than for the delinquency risk set. As before, F ratios were all significant at the 1 per cent level, but there was noticeable improvement in both the coefficients of determination and in the Lorenz curves. "Explained" variation (R^2) rose to about 13 per cent for the USSLL equation, to nearly 7 per cent for the MBA, and to just over 10 per cent for the NAMSB. The more dramatic improvement, however, was in the Lorenz curves. In the USSLL version, for example, the lowest quartile of loans as ranked by the risk index contained only about 1 per cent of the loans in foreclosure, and the lowest half only about 2 per cent (Chart 11). In fact, the index had to rise to the point where 90 per cent of all loans were included before the proportion of foreclosures reached the 50 per cent mark. This kind of performance certainly could not have been inferred from the R^2 which we calculated for this equation, and is perhaps indicative of the pitfalls associated with that statistic. Our regression equations do not fit perfectly into the classical least-squares framework because of our use of dummy variables. Nevertheless, approaches such as ours have been standard in the literature for several years. We merely point out that the Lorenz tests indicate that when the usual assumptions do not hold, rather important discrepancies may arise.

While the same independent variables were used in the foreclosure risk equations as in the delinquency risk set, we had no reason to believe that they would behave in the same way. There is no a priori basis for regarding loans in foreclosure merely as delinquents viewed at a later point in time. In fact, most loans which become seriously delinquent subsequently are restored to current status. It seems likely, therefore, that there are important differences between delinquents, per se, and loans which ultimately result in foreclosure. This point is

CHART 11

Lorenz Curves, Delinquent vs. Foreclosures, Individual

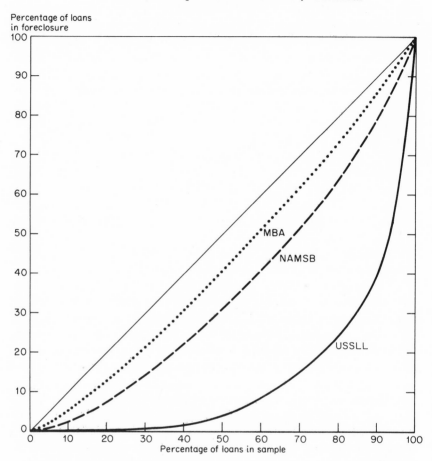

Percentage of loans
in foreclosure

Percentage of loans in sample

SOURCE: Appendix Tables B20–B22.

underscored above by our findings concerning the discriminating power of the equations. The improved estimates of the foreclosure risk equations is clear evidence that at least some of the variables we used are better predictors of foreclosure (given that delinquency has occurred) than of delinquency.

Loan-to-value ratio, as in the case of the delinquency equations, was directly related to risk. The coefficient was positive in all three equations and, except in the USSLL version, was significantly greater than zero. Term to maturity also yielded positive coefficients, but only one of these (USSLL) was significant at the 5 per cent level. In the NAMSB and MBA cases, t values were just short of the critical levels. The fact that both of these variables yielded positive signs emphasizes the inherent risks in low-equity loans. Small initial equities coupled with slower buildups (through stretched-out maturities) almost certainly pose substantial foreclosure hazards once a default has taken place.

The coefficients for payment-to-income ratio did not differ significantly from zero, except in the USSLL version, where it carried a positive sign. It would seem, however, that the fact that all the coefficients were algebraically larger than they were in the delinquency risk equations is not without significance. A priori, one would expect this kind of pattern if the variable serves at all to measure financial burden. Once a loan has slipped into the seriously delinquent category (by being three or more payments in arrears), it should be more difficult for the borrower to continue to make regular payments *and* make up the ones he has missed than to merely keep his payments current. If this is the case, one would expect larger risk coefficients for the foreclosure than for the delinquency equations.

Among the occupational groups there was less differentiation than in the delinquency risk equations, and the patterns that did emerge were quite at variance with the earlier results. For example, salesmen, who had been uniformly high risk in the delinquency case, yielded low risk coefficients for foreclosure in both the MBA and NAMSB equations (both were significant). Conversely, executives and managers, who had been among the better risks in the delinquency equations, provided the only significant coefficient in the USSLL foreclosure equation, but at the high-risk end of the spectrum. The other groups were pretty well clustered near the center, with the relative sizes of the coefficients varying from equation to equation. In contrast to the earlier results, therefore, it would be difficult to argue that there is any discernible relationship between occupational skill level and foreclosure risk.

Number of dependents and borrower age appeared to have little systematic effect on foreclosure risk, although some of the coefficients were significant at the 1 per cent level. The pattern appeared to be more or less random, however, with one possible exception. Very large families (eight or more dependents) yielded high risk coefficients in all three samples, and two of these were significantly greater than zero. This suggests that, within the usual family size limits, little distinction arises between delinquent loans and those in foreclosure; but that once the family becomes unusually large, foreclosure risks increase substantially. Marital status did not contribute significantly to the foreclosure risk. Both USSLL and NAMSB versions yielded lower coefficients for married than for unmarried borrowers, but none of these estimates were statistically significant.

Loan purpose (available only in the USSLL sample) again proved to be highly significant, as did junior financing. Loans for refinancing, as before, yielded a large risk coefficient, but the highest risk is associated with construction loans. This tends to confirm a belief long held by lenders that builder loans pose substantially higher than average foreclosure risks. Given the earlier finding that construction loans carry relatively high delinquency risks, the size of the foreclosure risk coefficient indicates that lenders' fears are well founded. What may be surprising, however, is the degree of risk associated with refinancing. This coefficient too was high for both the delinquency and foreclosure categories, suggesting that these loans are perhaps more hazardous than has heretofore been thought. Junior financing likewise appears to forebode ill, since the risk coefficient in the foreclosure equation is, as it was in the earlier version, quite high.

Regional coefficients, as was true in the delinquency equations, were highly significant, but are of little interest in themselves. Lender type, which applied only to the MBA equation, yielded a number of highly significant coefficients. Basically, they show that other things being equal, i.e. the other variables in the equation, the mortgage banker's chances of foreclosure are much less on loans serviced for commercial banks and individuals or on those held in his own account than they are for loans held for other financial intermediaries. Whether this finding reflects differences in foreclosure policies, types of loans for which the banker does servicing, or some other factor, we cannot say. It certainly doesn't imply that the *over-all* risk of foreclosure is higher for lenders other than commercial banks and individuals who leave the servicing to the mortgage banker. The higher risk interpretation once again applies only to the variables whose influence we specifically excluded. Loan type also proved to be a significant factor in the MBA equation, though not in the NAMSB. As was the case with delinquency risk, conventional loans carried the highest risk, followed by FHA's other than 203's, VA's, and FHA 203's. Differences between the latter three categories were not significant, but they all yielded significantly lower coefficients than conventionals.

POOLED EQUATIONS

As was true for the delinquency risk equations, pooling caused some loss in discriminating power. Nevertheless, *F* ratios for all the equations were well above rejection limits for significance at the 1 per cent level. Coefficients of determination were off somewhat, falling to 11 per cent for the USSLL, 5.5 per cent for the MBA, and 8.2 per cent for the NAMSB equation, but the percentage decline was not as great as in the delinquency equations. There was also a perceptible reduction in the area between the Lorenz curves and the reference line, although the USSLL equation continued to display very good discriminating power (Chart 12).

CHART 12

Lorenz Curves, Delinquent vs. Foreclosures, Pooled

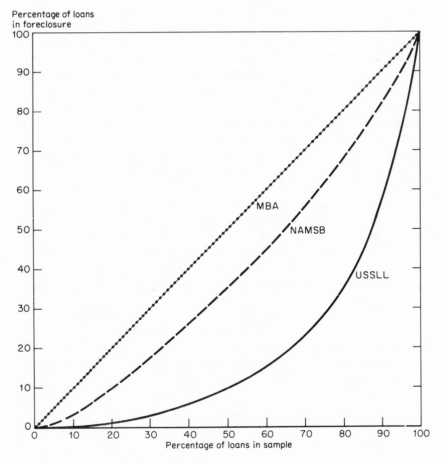

Percentage of loans
in foreclosure

Percentage of loans in sample

SOURCE: Appendix Tables B23–B25.

Loan-to-value ratio and term to maturity continued to show a positive correlation with risk, but with some loss in significance. The loan-to-value ratio, which had been highly significant in the MBA and NAMSB individual versions, met the 5 per cent criterion in only NAMSB after pooling. The term-to-maturity variable was significant (at the 1 per cent level) only in the USSLL version. While these results do not lend great support to the findings for the individual versions, they certainly do not contradict them.

The payment-to-income ratio coefficient was positive in two of the three equations (USSLL and MBA), but only one of these (USSLL) was significant. The NAMSB coefficient, as in the individual version, was negative but not significant. Again the evidence would seem to support the contention that this variable probably does a better job of measuring financial burden for foreclosure risk than for delinquency.

With but two exceptions, the remaining variables closely followed the patterns already commented upon for the individual versions of the equations. The exceptions, both in the MBA equation, occurred in the marital status and loan-type coefficients. Marital status, in the earlier version, yielded a lower value for single than for married borrowers, but the difference was not significant. This time the order was reversed, even though the coefficient just fell short of the critical level for significance. The result still leaves marital status in the doubtful category as far as significance is concerned, but would indicate that if a relationship does exist, married borrowers are probably less risky than single. As was the case with the delinquency equations, combining FHA 203's and other FHA's appeared to destroy the value of the loan-type variable. None of the coefficients was significant in the pooled version (where they had been in the individual), and the coefficient for conventional loans ranked between FHA's and VA's. These results are parallel to those for the NAMSB (where no breakdown of FHA's was employed).

STRAIGHT FORECLOSURE RISK: CURRENT LOANS
VERSUS LOANS IN FORECLOSURE

As was pointed out at the beginning of the foreclosure risk discussion, the previous two sections can be viewed as providing useful measures of the *conditional* probability of foreclosure, given that a loan is already in default. The present section, however, focuses upon the *unconditional* probability of foreclosure, and does so by matching the characteristics of current loans against the characteristics of loans in foreclosure. Since the USSLL data provided uniformly better results in the equations discussed above, it was decided to rely exclusively on that sample for developing the tests in this section. The decision was based in part on consideration of computation expense and in part on a desire to keep the arguments as straightforward as possible. Our previous results lead us to believe that our conclusions would not be substantially altered by the introduction of additional equations.

The discriminating power of estimated relationship was, on the whole, quite good. The F ratio was clearly significant at the 1 per cent level, even though it was numerically smaller than some of the others. The coefficient of determination was also lower, accounting for only about 5 per cent of the variation. The Lorenz curve, however, indicates that both of these statistics have a downward bias. The curvature (Chart 13) is only slightly less than it was in the USSLL individual version of the conditional delinquency risk equation, and substantially greater than any of the others. It should be noted, for example, that the lowest quartile of loans, as ranked by risk index value, contained less than 1 per cent of the loans in foreclosure. The lowest half only contained about 11 per cent of the foreclosures, and the lowest three-quarters only about 23 per cent. It would be erroneous, therefore, to place much weight on the low value of the R^2 statistic.

While there were no particular surprises in the signs of the coefficients, some of the variables which we had expected to be significant did not turn out that way. Loan-to-value ratio, payment-to-income ratio, occupation, marital status, and number of dependents all failed the tests, and borrower age yielded only one significant coefficient. It is worth noting that loan-to-value ratio and payment-to-income ratio both yielded positive coefficients, but only the former was anywhere near the required level for significance. Term to maturity, however, yielded a rather large positive coefficient and was significant at the 1 per cent level.

Once again loan purpose and junior financing were the key indicators of risk, the latter provided by far the highest coefficient and correlation with the dependent variable. Construction loans continued to lead loans for all other purposes in terms of contribution to risk, but refinancing and repair were not far behind. Home purchase remained at the low-risk end of the spectrum, and by a significant amount. Regional coefficients also yielded highly significant differences, again emphasizing the need to isolate such influences whenever possible. It is almost certain that some of the other relationships we estimated would have come out differently had this variable not been allowed for.

In general, these results follow the pattern one would expect from examining the coefficients in the current vs. noncurrent and delinquent

CHART 13

Lorenz Curve, Current vs. Foreclosures, USSLL

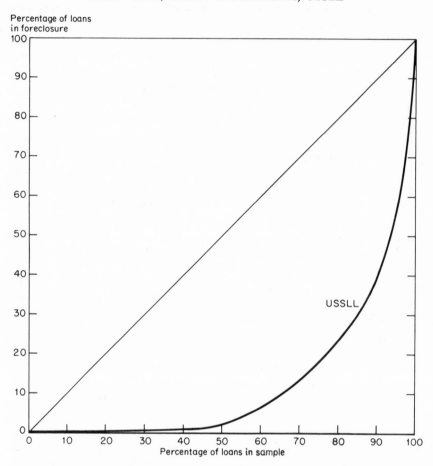

SOURCE: Appendix Table B26.

vs. foreclosure equations. That is, the coefficients in the present equation tended to fall between the coefficients for the earlier versions. Thus, if the signs on the previous equations differed, the sign for the current vs. foreclosure equation could be either plus or minus, depending on which of the two risks, delinquency or conditional foreclosure, dominated. Where the signs were the same on the earlier versions, the present equation yielded a coefficient whose *sign* confirmed that, but whether or not the coefficient was significant depended on the strength of the earlier relationships. Thus, for example, while loan-to-value ratio was significant in the delinquent vs. in foreclosure equation, it was not in the current vs. noncurrent, and this latter relationship dominated in the current vs. in foreclosure. The usefulness of the latter equation is underscored both by its evident discriminating power and by its ability to draw out such relationships.

III

The Postwar Course of Home Mortgage Quality

One of the two main objectives of this study was to ascertain what has happened to the quality of home mortgage credit over the postwar years. Some aspects of this problem have already been considered in Chapter I. It will be recalled that both delinquency and foreclosure remained at historically low levels throughout the late 1940's and early and middle 1950's. Delinquency rates began to rise perceptibly in the late 1950's, with more serious delinquency registering a sharper upsurge than casual delinquency. Foreclosure rates did not begin to turn up until 1960, but between then and 1963 they rose quite rapidly.

These, however, are strictly measures of performance. Could this deteriorating performance have been predicted at the time the loans were made? What has happened to "ex ante" quality as a result of changes in loan and borrower characteristics?

We have already noted in Chapter I that there were substantial changes in both borrower and loan characteristics during the years following World War II, but we made no attempt to relate these changes systematically to changes in performance. There have been numerous warnings that continued liberalization of mortgage terms was creating riskier loans. Just how much riskier, and what specific factors were creating the risks, however, was never made clear. It has been widely assumed, for example, that higher loan-to-value ratios and longer terms to maturity create greater hazards (a) because initial equities are lower, and (b) because the period during which the borrower has little equity in his property is lengthened. Presumably the argument would be that in a prolonged period of low equity, economic reversals are more likely to strike the borrower, who, having little vested interest, will let loan payments lapse. It is not obvious, however, that the fact that a borrower has only a small equity in his home will cause him to default on his loan. It is perhaps more likely that he defaults simply because he cannot afford to keep up the payments. Clearly this question requires careful analysis.

A second effect of liberalized terms is to magnify the borrower's resources. Lower down payments mean that given liquid assets are capable of purchasing either more home or more of other economic goods. Longer terms mean lower monthly payments for a given loan, or more loan for the same monthly payment. In either case, the borrower's ability to command goods and services with a given income is enlarged. But does this increase or reduce the danger of delinquency and foreclosure? Similar uncertainty surrounds the effects of other variables we examined.

To reduce or eliminate this uncertainty was the purpose of our regression studies in the previous chapter. We set out to test alternative sets of hypotheses to see which were consistent with the empirical evidence. We do not wish to minimize the difficulties, already noted, concerning those tests, but it does seem that they provide a useful framework from which to consider how changing loan and borrower characteristics influenced the quality of mortgage credit. What we propose to do in this chapter is to combine our cross-sectional regression results with the observed changes in loan and borrower characteristics in order to construct a time series "index" of mortgage quality.

Initially we had hoped to include most, if not all, of the variables used in our regressions in constructing such an index. This, however, did not prove practicable. As indicated in Chapter I, reliable time series of some of the variables we used are virtually nonexistent. While some data on mortgage borrower income, age, marital status, family size and occupation are available, they are much too sketchy (and in the wrong form) to be employed in regression equations. Information on loan-to-value ratios, monthly payment-to-income ratios, and term to maturity was as comprehensive as we would have liked, but left something to be desired from the standpoint of reliability. Various series were begun at different times, and the universes to which they apply are not always the ones we would like to work with. Most disconcerting of all is the fact that as the series have been revised, substantial differences show up in the years in which the revisions take effect.

In view of the apparently strong influence of junior financing found in our regressions, it is unfortunate that there is, insofar as we know, no data at all on the extent to which it has been used to supplement conventional home mortgage loans in the postwar years. We did make use of the Federal Home Loan Bank Board's series showing loan purpose, but this unfortunately covers all loans at savings and loan associations, thus including multifamily and commercial conventional loans and all types of VA and FHA loans, as well as conventional loans on one- to four-family residences. Furthermore, the FHLBB breakdown comprises only three categories of loans—those for construction, purchase, and "all other" purposes.

In view of the deficiencies of the published data, we had hoped (albeit faintly) that it would be possible for us to develop our own time series by stratifying our cross-sectional data by year of mortgage initiation. This proved to be feasible only on a limited scale. The biggest problem was the foreshortening of the age distribution of the loans in the samples. Attrition had taken its toll on lenders' portfolios, so that loans made in the late 1940's or early 1950's had, in many cases, been repaid before the sample was drawn. In other instances, sampling procedures mitigated against the probability of drawing older loans. In both the MBA and NAMSB surveys, the procedure was to first draw a sample of delinquent loans and then match these with a sample of current loans having the same age distribution. Since the vast majority of delinquencies take place between the second and seventh year after a loan is put on the books, the likelihood of including loans made before 1957 was greatly reduced. (Because of the scarcity of observations in these earlier years, it was not possible to include variables which contained more than a few dummy classes if we were to avoid the problems associated with empty cells in our classification matrix. It was, of course, possible to combine observations over several years, and this was done for the 1940's, but this device could not be employed extensively without destroying the time-series character of the data.)

Given the nature of these difficulties, it seemed advisable to adopt a compromise solution. Instead of using the full complement of variables, we based our indexes on at most five: loan-to-value ratio, term to maturity, payment-to-income ratio, loan purpose, and junior financing. Separate calculations were made for VA, FHA, and conventional loans, for published (aggregate) time series and the time series derived from our samples, and for delinquency risk (current vs. noncurrent status), conditional foreclosure risk (delinquent vs. in foreclosure), and straight foreclosure risk (current vs. in foreclosure). Altogether, we computed fourteen different time series, using intermediate versions of the equations discussed in the last chapter.[1]

For conventional loans the equations were derived solely from the USSLL data by regressing loan status on loan-to-value ratio, term to maturity, loan purpose, and junior financing. Monthly payment-to-income ratio was dropped, in the case of conventional loans, because for them reliable data on how this variable changed over time were lacking. Loan purpose for the published data was based on a three-category classification (construction, purchase, and "all other"), and for the time series constructed from the sample data on a four-category classification (construction, purchase, refinancing, and repair). Junior financing was not used in connection with the published data, since no time series relating to its incidence were available, but it does appear in the equation for the sample data.

The equations for both FHA and VA loans were derived from the NAMSB data alone by regressing loan status on loan-to-value ratio, term to maturity, and payment-to-income ratio. Identical versions were used for FHA and VA and for published and derived time series data. It will be recalled that we did not have information on loan purpose and junior financing in the NAMSB data. This presents no serious problem, however, with FHA and VA loans, since no secondary financing is permitted in connection with these loans and the vast majority of them are made for home purchase.

1. Results Using Published (Aggregate) Time Series

The data in Tables 12–14 were inserted into the regression equations listed in Appendix B to develop risk indexes of both delinquency and foreclosure for conventional, FHA, and VA loans. These indexes appear in Table 15 and Charts 14 and 15.

The reader is cautioned against trying to draw inferences from the relative sizes of the indexes for conventional loans as compared with the FHA's and VA's. A different equation was used for conventional loans and, since the regression coefficients depend in part on the proportion of loans in each status category in the cross-section sample, direct comparison could be very misleading. What can be compared, however, are changes in the indexes over time, and that is our primary objective. It is also possible to compare the absolute size of the VA

---

[1] A full description of the equations on which the indexes are based, together with relevant statistical tests and sample sizes, is contained in Appendix C.

TABLE 12

Time Series on Selected Variables for Conventional Loans at
Savings and Loan Associations, Aggregate Data, 1950-67

Year	(RLS) Loan-to-Value Ratio (per cent) (1)	(T) Term to Maturity (months) (2)	Percentage of Loans Made for:		
			(P_1) House Construction (3)	House Purchase (4)	(P_2) Other (5)
1950	66.9	160	33.7	42.9	23.4
1951	64.6	179	31.6	44.9	23.5
1952	65.6	181	31.8	44.7	23.5
1953	65.4	182	31.9	44.9	23.2
1954	66.8	187	34.3	42.9	22.8
1955	69.8	194	35.4	45.8	18.8
1956	69.8	196	35.8	44.7	19.5
1957	69.3	202	34.3	45.2	20.5
1958	70.8	211	33.2	42.5	24.3
1959	72.8	223	34.3	43.6	22.1
1960	73.6	229	32.7	42.9	24.4
1961	74.4	233	29.3	41.5	29.2
1962	75.8	250	28.8	41.1	30.1
1963	76.3	265	28.5	40.1	31.4
1964	75.6	277	26.6	42.4	31.0
1965	75.9	277	24.1	44.9	30.3
1966	74.1	269	21.6	46.3	32.1
1967	75.3	297	21.1	47.9	31.1

SOURCE: Through 1963 col. 1 is a simple average of cols. 5 and 6 in Table 2; col. 2 is a simple average of cols. 5 and 6 in Table 1. Cols. 3, 4, and 5 are taken from United States Savings and Loan League, *Savings and Loan Fact Book,* 1968, p. 87. From 1964 through 1967, cols. 1 and 2 are simple averages of data in Table 72, p. 91 of *Savings and Loan Fact Book,* 1968.

and FHA indexes, since the same equation was used for calculating both.

Except for a rather sharp drop from 1950 to 1951, the delinquency risk index for conventional loans displayed only slight variation over the period between 1951 and 1961. After 1961, however, there was a steady decline through 1967, except for a very minor rise in 1966. The highest values (excluding 1950) were reached in 1952, 1954, and 1961;

TABLE 13

Time Series on Selected Variables for Section 203 Loans
Insured by FHA, Aggregate Data, 1946-67

Year	Loan-to-Value Ratio (per cent) (1)	Term to Maturity (months) (2)	Payment-to-Income Ratio (per cent) (3)
1946	81.4	240	14.5
1947	79.2	235	15.0
1948	78.3	236	15.0
1949	80.1	256	15.5
1950	80.7	266	15.5
1951	78.0	266	14.5
1952	78.2	248	14.5
1953	80.2	252	15.0
1954	80.0	258	15.0
1955	83.6	290	15.0
1956	81.8	288	15.0
1957	82.4	288	15.0
1958	88.4	310	16.0
1959	90.4	324	16.0
1960	91.0	330	16.5
1961	91.8	337	16.5
1962	92.4	346	16.5
1963	92.6	353	16.5
1964	92.8	359	16.5
1965	92.7	362	16.0
1966	92.7	353	16.0
1967	92.4	350	16.0

SOURCE: Through 1964 col. 1 is a simple average of cols. 1 and 2 in Table 2. Col. 2 is a simple average of cols. 1 and 2 in Table 1. Col. 3 is a simple average of cols. 1 and 3 in Table 3. After 1964 the sources are the same as those in Tables 1, 2, and 3.

the lowest values in 1957, 1959, and the period after 1961. Differences were not great, however, until 1964 and it would be difficult to argue that either a cyclical pattern or a trend was in evidence before that time. The declines of 1964 and 1967 are another matter, clearly showing a substantial reduction in delinquency risk. The FHA delinquency risk index showed a little more cyclical variability but no long-

TABLE 14
*Time Series on Selected Variables for Primary Section 501
Loans Guaranteed by VA, Aggregate Data, 1946-67*

Year	Loan-to-Value Ratio (per cent) (1)	Term to Maturity (months) (2)	Payment-to-Income Ratio (per cent) (3)
1946	90.9	228	15.0[a]
1947	90.0	221	15.0[a]
1948	84.2	215	15.0[a]
1949	85.6	232	15.0[a]
1950	89.2	257	15.0[a]
1951	85.2	253	15.0[a]
1952	83.6	251	15.0[a]
1953	85.4	254	15.0[a]
1954	89.7	283	15.5
1955	91.4	299	15.0
1956	89.7	295	15.5
1957	89.0	292	16.5
1958	91.0	304	16.5
1959	92.8	314	16.5
1960	93.8	314	16.5
1961	95.1	326	16.5
1962	96.4	335	16.5
1963	96.7	340	16.5
1964	96.9	342	16.0[a]
1965	96.7	343	16.0[a]
1966	97.0	343	16.0[a]
1967	97.6	344	16.0[a]

SOURCE: Through 1964 col. 1 is a simple average of cols. 3 and 4 in Table 2. Col. 2 is a simple average of cols. 3 and 4 in Table 1. Col. 3 was computed from data supplied by the Veterans' Administration. After 1964 the sources are the same as those in Tables 1, 2 and 3.

[a]Estimated in order to provide comparability in the regression equations.

TABLE 15

Calculated Values for Risk Index, by Year, Aggregate Data, 1946-67

| | Delinquency | | | Conditional Foreclosure Risk | | | Straight Foreclosure Risk |
Year	Conventional Loans (1)	FHA Loans (2)	VA Loans (3)	Conventional Loans (4)	FHA Loans (5)	VA Loans (6)	Conventional Loans (7)
1946	—	.513	.567	—	.224	.238	—
1947	—	.506	.561	—	.213	.236	—
1948	—	.501	.539	—	.210	.216	—
1949	—	.497	.536	—	.223	.229	—
1950	.453	.495	.544	.277	.230	.247	.223
1951	.439	.484	.522	.285	.227	.239	.224
1952	.440	.494	.519	.286	.209	.231	.227
1953	.439	.501	.525	.287	.224	.238	.227
1954	.440	.496	.527	.292	.226	.263	.229
1955	.437	.495	.525	.296	.253	.280	.231
1956	.437	.488	.520	.298	.247	.270	.232
1957	.434	.491	.516	.300	.249	.262	.233
1958	.438	.504	.518	.306	.272	.274	.237
1959	.434	.505	.520	.314	.285	.282	.240
1960	.436	.504	.525	.317	.287	.285	.243
1961	.440	.504	.523	.319	.293	.299	.246
1962	.436	.502	.524	.329	.300	.307	.250
1963	.434	.499	.523	.338	.304	.311	.255
1964	.423	.496	.524	.342	.307	.313	.242
1965	.422	.495	.523	.340	.311	.313	.242
1966	.424	.499	.524	.333	.306	.314	.238
1967	.411	.500	.526	.348	.307	.310	.245

SOURCE: Index values were calculated by inserting the data in Tables 12-14 into the regression equations listed in Appendix C. For definition of the risk indexes, see Chapter II, Section 1.

74

CHART 14

Delinquency Risk, Aggregate Data

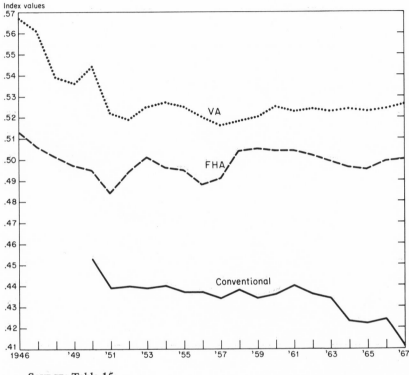

SOURCE: Table 15.

term trend. The highest value was recorded in 1946, the lowest in 1951. The lowest value at the end of the period (1965), however, was higher than either of the previous lows (1951 and 1956) perhaps indicating some upward drift in the series. There was some evidence that cyclical movements in the FHA delinquency risk index followed conditions in the money and capital markets. For example, the index declined steadily through 1951, rose in 1952 and 1953, declined through 1956, rose from 1957 through 1960, and declined again through 1965.

Disregarding the years 1946–49, which were missing from the conventional series, and the period after 1961 (when the risk on conventionals improved) the VA delinquency risk index behaved very much like the one for conventional loans. Variability after 1950 was slight, and no obvious patterns are evident. There was a rather sub-

CHART 15

Foreclosure Risk, Aggregate Data

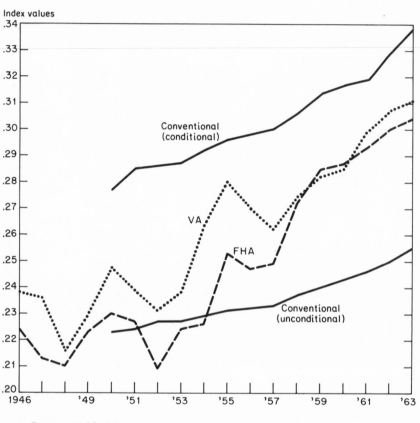

stantial decline in the index, however, between 1946 and 1952, when a drop from .567 to .519 was recorded. It is perhaps noteworthy that the VA index remained above the FHA for the entire postwar period, although the spread narrowed slightly in 1957 and 1958.

In contrast to the delinquency risk indexes, those measuring foreclosure risk (both conditional and straight) showed a definite upward trend over most of the postwar period. The indexes for conventional loans rose steadily until 1963 for straight foreclosure and 1964 for conditional. With regard to conditional foreclosure risk (the risk of foreclosure, given that a loan is delinquent), 1967 showed the largest rise followed by 1959, 1962, and 1963. The only years when the index declined were 1965 and 1966. Unconditional foreclosure risk increased most from 1958 through 1963, with the greatest single year's gain in the period being recorded in the latter year. The rise of 1967, however, which followed declines in 1964–66, was sharper even than the one experienced in 1963.

The conditional foreclosure risk index for FHA loans stood at about the same level in 1954 as that at which it started in 1946, although it had fluctuated somewhat in the interim. After 1954, however, it rose considerably, with much of the rise coming in two years—1955 and 1958. The later years, 1959–67, were marked by a gradual but persistent increase (except for a slight decline in 1966), and this gradual drift pushed the index well above its earlier levels.

The VA conditional foreclosure risk index showed a pattern very much like that of the FHA, although it jumped considerably in 1954— one year earlier than the beginning of the upward surge of the FHA index. It also appears that, except for two years (1959 and 1960), delinquent VA loans carried higher risks of foreclosure than FHA.

In general, the results of working with published time series seem to indicate that there was no particular trend in delinquency risk over the postwar period, although cyclical variations are in evidence. Risks on conventionals clearly declined after 1961. Looking at foreclosure risk, however, it would appear that once a loan has become delinquent, the chances that it will wind up in foreclosure have increased markedly over the years for all types of loans (the improvement in conventionals between 1964 and 1966 was more than offset by the rise in risks in 1967). Also, a direct comparison of FHA and VA loans would indicate that the latter are slightly more risky than the former. This spread, however, appears to have narrowed considerably in recent years. Finally, straight foreclosure risk (available only on conventionals) rose considerably between 1950 and 1963, declined through 1966, and rose sharply in 1967. This latter rise, however, still left the index somewhat below its 1963 peak.

We must confess that we were somewhat surprised by the behavior of the delinquency risk indexes. We had expected that they, like the foreclosure risk indexes, would move upward through the period. The obvious statistical explanation of why they did not is that the persistent lengthening of term to maturity (which showed a negative relationship to risk in the delinquency equations, but a positive relationship in the foreclosure equations) simply swamped the effects of the other variables. This fact, of course, underscores one of the dangers of trying to apply cross-sectional results to time series data. If, as was pointed out in the last chapter, the coefficient on the term to maturity variable is biased downward when other variables are dropped from the equation, the lengthening of maturities over time may have nothing whatever to do with changes in delinquency risk.

There are other methodological difficulties as well. Most of these center around the implicit assumption we made that the economic conditions which prevailed when the sample was drawn were equally relevant to the earlier years when the loans were made. Obviously just which loans are in trouble at any given moment is going to depend on how economic conditions affect different borrowers. If a different set of conditions would lead to a different pattern of delinquency and foreclosure, then our equations would not apply to a situation where economic conditions were different. Whether this weakness was, in fact, of sufficient importance to nullify our findings is impossible to say. The dangers are there, however, and we wish to emphasize that our findings should be interpreted with caution.

2. Results Using Time Series Derived from Sample Data

The time series derived from our sample data were employed for two purposes: (1) to check whether our sample was representative of all loans made in the same periods, and (2) to provide information on some variables, notably loan purpose and junior financing, for which published time series were inadequate or nonexistent. Obviously, the sample time series could not be extended beyond 1963, the year in which the sample was drawn. Comparison of Tables 16–18 with Tables 12–14 indicates that although there are some differences in the two sets of time series, there are basic similarities. The existing differences can probably be attributed to (1) the few cases in the derived time series where the sample size was too small to give reliable estimates, and (2) the averaging technique which was used in deriving the time series based on published data. Loan-to-value ratios and terms to maturity in that set are almost certainly understated as a result of taking a simple average of the values for loans on new and existing properties. In spite of this, however, the same general trends emerge in both sets of data.

This observation is borne out by the striking similarity in the behavior of the two sets of risk indexes (see Table 19 and Charts 16 and 17). There are, of course, some minor differences in the year-to-year fluctuations, but the over-all trends are very much the same. The

TABLE 16

USSLL Conventional Loans, Selected Variables, Sample Data, 1941-63

Year	(RLS) Loan-to-Value Ratio (per cent) (1)	(T) Term to Maturity (months) (2)	Percentage of Loans Extended for:				Percentage of Loans with Junior Financing (7)	Sample Size (8)
			(P₁) Construction (3)	Purchase (4)	(P₂) Repairs (5)	(P₃) Refinancing (6)		
1941-49	63.5	196	15.2	47.9	10.8	26.1	4.4	43
1950	60.7	196	19.4	41.7	13.9	25.0	3.1	40
1951	64.6	198	18.2	63.7	3.6	14.5	11.8	69
1952	63.6	195	24.0	55.9	8.6	11.5	16.4	117
1953	64.7	188	22.6	47.5	7.3	22.6	9.2	144
1954	63.2	194	21.4	51.6	7.5	19.5	11.1	183
1955	68.6	200	18.5	56.0	8.6	16.9	23.3	332
1956	67.7	196	21.3	45.8	7.1	25.8	17.7	431
1957	65.0	203	16.1	57.4	4.1	22.4	25.8	484
1958	67.5	213	17.7	49.0	5.5	27.8	25.2	744
1959	71.2	231	19.6	53.1	3.5	23.8	30.0	963
1960	71.2	234	15.1	56.7	3.7	24.5	25.7	936
1961	72.9	237	9.7	54.0	3.2	34.1	19.6	1,015
1962	75.1	253	8.5	54.5	3.2	33.8	20.2	694
1963	74.6	269	13.3	48.9	2.2	35.6	21.9	61

SOURCE: All figures were derived from the USSLL sample of 6,550 loans. The loans were stratified by year and the average calculated.

TABLE 17

MBA FHA Loans, Selected Variables, Sample Data, 1946-63

Year	Loan-to-Value Ratio (per cent) (1)	Term to Maturity (months) (2)	Payment-to-Income Ratio (per cent) (3)	Sample Size (4)
1946-49	80.7	289	17.2	17
1950	91.6	296	14.8	30
1951	84.4	279	13.4	14
1952	80.3	274	14.8	7
1953	85.0	279	13.9	22
1954	86.5	298	13.6	31
1955	88.5	296	14.1	67
1956	86.0	287	14.1	38
1957	87.8	295	15.3	58
1958	91.7	317	17.2	240
1959	93.2	334	16.8	360
1960	93.7	342	17.3	353
1961	94.7	342	17.0	310
1962	95.4	336	16.7	186
1963	92.9	340	17.5	14

SOURCE: All figures were derived from the MBA sample of 3,832 loans. The loans were stratified by year and the average calculated.

only substantial difference is in the delinquency risk index for conventional loans. This can be attributed to the reformulation of the regression equation in this case, in order to take account of the finer breakdown of loan purpose and the addition of the junior financing variable made possible by the sample data. This reformulation, which was certainly an improvement, resulted in a definite upward trend in the index over time. It is significant that up to 1954 there were only minor fluctuations in the index, but that afterward, especially in 1958 and 1959, greater risks were clearly in evidence. The index tapered off somewhat after 1959, but it remained well above the 1954 level. These results are entirely consistent with the behavior of published delinquency rates in the same period.

The FHA delinquency risk index from the sample data was at the same level in 1963 as in 1951, again indicating that there was probably no trend toward either higher or lower quality in the FHA loans made over these years. There were, however, as in the index based on published data, substantial year-to-year fluctuations, with peaks being reached in 1950, 1955, 1958, and 1962. All of these years, it might be noted, fell in the latter stages of periods of monetary ease. The VA index again registered a substantial decline in the early years, dropping from .568 for the 1946–49 period to .522 in 1953. After that time, just as in the version based on published data, it remained relatively stable. Again it should be noted that the VA risk index remained above the FHA, except for one year (1958) when they were virtually equal.

Conditional foreclosure risk again registered clear upward trends in all cases, but the pattern was slightly different from that found by use of the aggregative published data. Conditional foreclosure risk for conventional loans was almost identical to the previous results, except that in the earlier version it advanced somewhat in 1960, whereas the sample version shows a decline. The over-all gain for the entir₋ period was almost identical. The straight foreclosure risk index for

TABLE 18

MBA VA Loans, Selected Variables, Sample Data, 1946-63

Year	Loan-to-Value Ratio (per cent) (1)	Term to Maturity (months) (2)	Payment-to-Income Ratio (per cent) (3)	Sample Size (4)
1946-49	97.4	265	16.5	29
1950	98.0	290	15.2	48
1951	93.2	303	14.1	27
1952	91.7	278	15.1	22
1953	91.4	304	14.5	34
1954	96.2	329	16.0	138
1955	94.1	322	16.0	168
1956	92.9	321	16.5	182
1957	93.6	317	15.6	96
1958	95.3	349	16.2	65
1959	98.7	353	16.7	171
1960	99.3	346	17.1	131
1961	99.6	351	16.8	128
1962	99.0	352	17.2	149
1963	99.0	354	17.5	20

SOURCE: All figures were derived from the MBA sample of 3,832 loans. The loans were stratified by year and the average calculated.

TABLE 19

Calculated Values of Risk Index, by Year, Sample Data, 1946-63

| Year | Delinquency Risk | | | Conditional Foreclosure Risk | | | Straight Foreclosure Risk |
	Conventional Loans (1)	FHA Loans (2)	VA Loans (3)	Conventional Loans (4)	FHA Loans (5)	VA Loans (6)	Conventional Loans (7)
1946-49	.410	.480	.568	.271	.233	.273	.223
1950	.407	.527	.559	.273	.260	.294	.223
1951	.399	.506	.531	.271	.258	.292	.224
1952	.415	.489	.537	.278	.236	.270	.228
1953	.417	.508	.522	.267	.257	.285	.226
1954	.410	.505	.528	.275	.273	.305	.226
1955	.436	.514	.523	.287	.275	.295	.234
1956	.439	.508	.518	.287	.263	.288	.233
1957	.436	.510	.524	.287	.266	.293	.234
1958	.447	.514	.513	.298	.279	.311	.238
1959	.447	.512	.526	.312	.294	.320	.244
1960	.438	.509	.532	.306	.297	.318	.241
1961	.441	.514	.531	.305	.302	.322	.239
1962	.440	.520	.527	.314	.302	.317	.242
1963	.440	.506	.526	.327	.293	.318	.246

SOURCE: Index values were calculated by inserting the data in Tables 16-18 into the regression equations listed in Appendix C. For definition of the risk indexes see Chapter II, Section 1.

CHART 16

Delinquency Risk, Sample Data

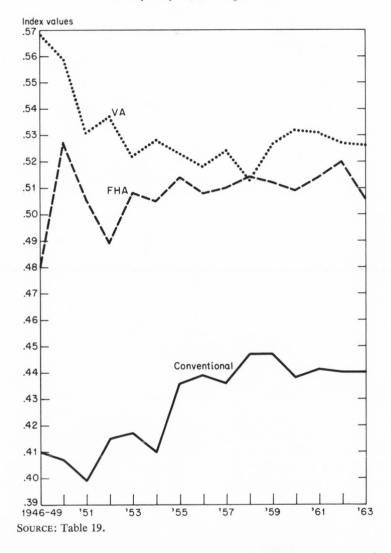

SOURCE: Table 19.

conventional loans behaved in an almost identical manner for both sets of data until the last three years, when the sample-based version lagged behind. Most of the discrepancy in that case can be attributed to the year 1961, which saw the two indexes moving in opposite directions.

CHART 17

Foreclosure Risk, Sample Data

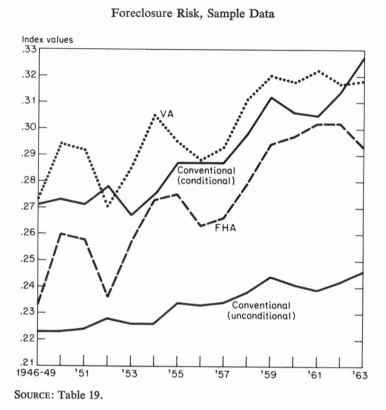

SOURCE: Table 19.

The FHA conditional foreclosure index, which for the published data had remained low through the mid-1950's, advancing only in the later years, in the sample version began to rise earlier (1953). The over-all trend was much the same, however, the highest values being reached in the late years of the period. The same thing was true for the VA index, with substantial increases being recorded in the early years, followed by an additional upward surge from 1958 to 1963. The fact that the sample VA and FHA loans showed increased fore-closure risk earlier than the population of all such loans may be due to the fact that the sample loans were drawn entirely from mortgage bankers' portfolios. It is possible (indeed probable) that mortgage bankers liberalized terms earlier than other lenders. It is also possible, however, that the differences primarily reflect the influence of averaging technique commented upon earlier.

In general, the results provide fairly conclusive evidence that there has been some deterioration of mortgage quality over the postwar period. If one makes allowances for the possibility of a wrong sign on term to maturity, the effect of which is considerable, it is likely that a slight upward drift in delinquency risk took place. There is no question that there was a substantial increase in foreclosure risk, whether measured as the probability that a delinquent loan would wind up in foreclosure or as the probability that a "typical" current loan would meet the same fate. The trends are simply too strong to conclude otherwise.

3. Comparison of the Risk Indexes with Published Delinquency and Foreclosure Rates

The risk indexes developed in this study refer only to *new* loans being made at various dates, whereas published delinquency and foreclosure rates are for *outstanding* loans in lenders' portfolios. The relationship between our calculated indexes and published delinquency and foreclosure rates partly depends, therefore, on the age distribution of loans in lenders' portfolios. Moreover, actual delinquency and foreclosure rates are influenced by economic conditions prevailing at the time the loans are outstanding. Hence they may change by more or less than the index, or may even move in the opposite direction.

There are, unfortunately, no published data on the characteristics of loans outstanding from which a risk index for outstanding loans could be calculated. Nor are there any empirical data available on the changing age composition of lenders' portfolios. Attempts to simulate portfolio quality by assuming no change in the age composition of loans and using published data on the characteristics of new loans proved fruitless. An earlier point that bears repeating is that if more definite conclusions are to be drawn about temporal changes in mortgage quality, it will be necessary to work with inter-temporal samples of terminated loans.

Appendix A

Sampling Techniques, Questionnaires, and Worksheets

United States Savings and Loan League Data

PARTICIPATING INSTITUTIONS

In selecting a sample of savings associations for the delinquency study the League aimed at a cross section of the business that would reflect primarily geographic patterns of delinquency. No attempt was made to include size or other institutional differences except within the geographic framework. The basis for the regional distribution of delinquencies was reports from associations to the League's Data Exchange Group (now called the MIRRORS group).

Originally 100 institutions were invited to participate in the study. Of that group fifty responded favorably, but attrition and difficulties with the schedule as set up reduced the final group to thirty-eight. In making up the original list, only associations which were large enough to have at least 100 delinquency accounts were included.

INSTRUCTION SHEETS: DELINQUENCIES ON SINGLE-FAMILY
CONVENTIONAL LOANS AT SAVINGS AND LOAN ASSOCIATIONS

Note: This study is restricted to conventional single-family home loans. FHA and VA loans and loans on multiple-family properties are *not to be included* in the sample.

We recognize that variations exist in loan procedures from one association to another. Because of this fact, it is difficult to establish rigid guidelines for this study. Therefore, we will cite the principles we wish to hold to in the study and follow with a recommended, but illustrative, method of proceeding. The officers supervising the local work can then determine the most efficient method of getting the job done in their own shop. We ask only that the person assigned to extract the information from the loan files have working familiarity with the loan records and procedures and not be simply a clerk. He, or she, should review thoroughly the information in these instructions.

I. *Defining a Delinquent Loan*

A delinquent loan is defined as a loan in arrearage sixty days or more. The loan is sixty days or more delinquent if the borrower owes the equivalent of two monthly payments in the last twelve months. You may follow the local practice regarding partial loan payments. *What we wish to guard against is including thirty day-past due loans in our sample.*

II. *Drawing the Sample*

A. Select at random 100 loans from the delinquent loan file. To insure randomness, each eligible loan must have an equal chance of being included in the study. Determine first the number of loans *eligible* for the study. Remember to *exclude* the ineligible FHA, VA and multi-unit property loans. If the number is 100 or less, include every loan. If the number exceeds 100, you must sample systematically. If the number of loans is 150, e.g., include two loans and skip each third loan. If your association has 300 delinquent loans, select one out of every three loans from a register or a listing of such loans, or use the assembled ledger cards and select every third card. If the association had 350 delinquent loans, you would select two loans and skip five loans, etc. It may be that this sampling could best be done in the Collections Department.

B. Select at random 100 loans from the current loan file. If you have 7,000 loans on the books, then the sampling ratio would be 100/7000, or one out of 70. Typically, you would work through a loan register, a similar listing, or the loan file itself and select every nth loan, record the number of that account and include it in the study. The account numbers of the loans included in the survey may be recorded on a separate sheet, or directly on Worksheet A. Remember, however, to keep the delinquent loans and the current loans separate, because Worksheet B applies only to delinquent loans.

III. *Definitions—Worksheet A*

Worksheet A is to be prepared from materials in the loan file for all loans included in the survey—current and delinquent. All replies

TABLE A1
WORKSHEET A:
DELINQUENCY STUDY—CONVENTIONAL SINGLE-FAMILY MORTGAGES

Name of Assn. _____ _____# of Loan _____ Delinquent _____

Location of Property _____ _____ Current _____

(In City _____; Built-Up Suburb _____; New Surburban Development _____)
Check Appropriate Boxes or Fill in Blanks:

1. Loan Terms:
Date Loan Closed* _____ / _____ / _____
Original Balance $_____
Interest Rate _____ %

Service Charge* $_____

Monthly Payment (PI)* $_____

2. Type of Loan:*
_____ Original Borrower—Walk-in
_____ Original Borrower—Brought in by Broker
_____ Builder loan—assumed
_____ Builder loan—substitued
_____ Ordinary assumption
_____ Ordinary substitution

3. Loan and Property Characteristics:
Purchase Price of Home $_____
Appraisal $_____
Downpayment* $_____
Maturity of Loan _____
Any Junior Financing?* Yes _____ No _____
Pledged Saving Acct. _____
Other (Describe) _____

Age of Home:*
New _____
Used: 0 to 5 yrs. _____
5 to 10 yrs. _____
10 to 15 yrs. _____
16 and Over _____

4. Age of Head of Household:
_____ 21 to 29
_____ 30 to 34
_____ 35 to 39
_____ 40 to 44
_____ 45 to 49
_____ 50 to 54
_____ 55 to 59
_____ 60 & over

5. Marital Status:
Married _____
Widowed _____
Divorced _____
Single _____

6. Number of Dependents: _____

Number of Jobs* _____

Length of Time on
Main Job _____

89

7. Annual Income:
Husband $ _____ /year. . . . . ☐ Wages and Salary   ☐ Own Business   ☐ Other
Wife $ _____ /year. . . . . ☐ Wages and Salary   ☐ Own Business   ☐ Other
Other $ _____ /year. . . . . __ From _____
Other $ _____ /year. . . . . __ From _____

8. Occupation:
__ Self-employed
__ Executive or Manager
__ Salesman
__ White-collar
__ Skilled Labor
__ Unskilled Labor
__ Other (Farmer, Military, etc.)

9. Purpose of Loan:*
__ Construction
__ Purchase
__ Repair and Improvement
__ Refinancing
__ Other (Specify) _____

10. Credit Information:
__ No Credit Report
__ Credit Info. by Bureau _____
__ Credit Info. by Assn. _____
__ No. Jobs past 5 yrs. _____
__ Length of Time in State _____

Balance Sheet Info: Yes _____ No _____
Court Items: Yes _____ No _____
Collections: Yes _____ No _____
Rating Given Borrower by Loan Interviewer:*
__ Excellent   __ Fair
__ Satisfactory   __ Poor
                   __ None

11. Reference Information (Check applicable items):
__ No References Given
__ Trade-Retailers & Merchants
__ Auto Finance Company
__ Small Loan Company
__ Bank and Mortgage Items

__ Private Party
Complete:
__ Number of References Given
__ Number Checked

Other Comments: _____

_____

_____

*Instructions Define These Terms

March 1963

90

must be facts available to loan officer at time of loan application, approval, or closing. Remember to indicate whether each loan is *current* or *delinquent* in the upper right-hand corner of the worksheet.

Location of Property. Place here the address of the property. This item is important for identification purposes. We ask, if possible, that a loan officer classify the loans as "In City," "Built-up Suburb," or "New Suburban Development."

Item 1. *Date loan closed.* Refers to date borrower incurred contractual liability to association—the date of loan closing for construction loans.

Service charge. Includes total of fees and charges, paid by borrower, whether itemized or not. Credit report, appraisal, and title fees are included. Enter dollar amount.

Monthly payment. Includes principal and interest. Escrow payments are not included in this item.

Item 2. *Type of loan:*

Original borrower—brought in by broker. Borrower referred to association by real estate agent or builder.

Builder loan—assumed. Borrower assumed loan made originally to homebuilder.

Builder loan—substituted. Borrower's loan, although a new contract, was closely tied to (substituted for) the builder's original loan on the same property.

Ordinary assumption. Borrower assumed loan made originally to another borrower.

Ordinary substitution. Borrower's loan, although a new contract, was tied closely to (substituted for) an earlier loan made by association to another borrower on the same property.

Item 3. *Downpayment.* The earnest money payment and other cash transferred from buyer to seller. Item should appear on settlement statement.

Any junior financing? Any additional borrowing to get the downpayment or any additional collateral offered to make the first mortgage possible. This can be by builder or other third party as well as borrower. Includes pledged savings account, notes, or agreements of builders, or any outside party. Answer "yes" or "no." Where loan file provides evidence that junior financing existed, indicate type of secondary financing involved.

New home. Refers to home not previously occupied.
Used home. Previously occupied property.

Items 4, 5, 6 and 8. Refer to Head of Household.

Number of jobs. Refers to "moonlighting" by borrower.

Item 7. *Annual income.* Indicate dollar amount and whether total comes from wages and salary, own business, or other sources. If income of persons other than husband or wife were noted, indicate source of such income.

Item 9. *Purpose of loan:*

Construction. Refers to long-term construction loan to borrower.

Purchase. Home purchase. Also includes builder loans that have been assumed or substituted by the home owner.

Repair and improvement. Loan where indicated purpose is major alteration or improvement of property.

Refinancing. Loan written to repay or recast an existing home mortgage debt, even if additional funds are granted for other purposes.

Items 10 & 11. *Credit information.* Practice here will vary, depending on degree of reliance on outside credit agency. Recommend that loan application and credit report be used *together* in completing sections 10 and 11.

Rating by loan interviewer. Where a rating appears in loan file in writing, indicate evaluation. Where it does not, check "None."

Number of references given and number checked. Item refers to credit work done by association. Reply requires a counting of references and a counting of the number checked.

IV. *Definitions—Worksheet B.* (For delinquent loans only).

Present loan balance. As of March 1, 1963. Taken from loan ledger card.

Number of payments in arrears. As of March 1, 1963. See definition of delinquent loan at beginning of instructions. Partial payments are to be handled according to association practice. If more than 50 per cent of a payment is overdue, most associations count this as a missed payment.

Reason for delinquency. As ascertained in Collections Department.

Attitude of borrower. Indicate in capsule fashion essence of any report or reports noted on records by collections personnel regarding contact with borrower.

TABLE A2
WORKSHEET B:
DELINQUENCY STUDY–CONVENTIONAL SINGLE-FAMILY MORTGAGES
(To be Prepared by Collections Dept.)

Name of Assn. _____ # of Loan _____

Present Loan Balance $ _____ No. Payments in Arrears _____

Payment Experience:

____ Problems throughout loan life

____ Intermittent trouble

____ Good until recently, then

____ no payment

____ Other (_____)

Reason for Delinquency:

____ Improper regard for obligations

____ Curtailment of income

____ Excessive obligations

____ Death or illness

____ Marital difficulties

____ Other reasons: _____

Attitude of borrower when contacted: _____

_____

Other Comments: _____

_____

_____

_____

Other comments. Might include notation regarding previous collection problems and how resolved; comments regarding changes in borrower's situation since date of original loan.

V. *Other Instructions*

    A. Time schedule. If workload permits, records research should be conducted prior to March 15.

    B. Completed worksheets. Hold for visit of League Field Service Representative. He will review procedures followed and pick up the worksheets.

    C. Special procedures. If any are employed, please note these for us. Such notations will be of great help in the editing which will precede electronic processing.

Mortgage Bankers Association Data

PARTICIPATING INSTITUTIONS

The universe from which the sample was drawn consisted of the regular reporters in the MBA's quarterly delinquency survey. As of June 30, 1962, a year earlier than the actual survey date, there were 38 mutual savings banks, 102 commercial banks, and 256 mortgage companies so reporting. For each institution, a ratio was computed of the number of loans delinquent ninety days or more plus number of loans in foreclosure to the total number of loans serviced. This ratio was then used to compute variances and to estimate the required sample size for each of the three types of institution. The ratio was also used along with the number of loans in default to determine the within-institution sampling rate. The schedule was:

Loans in Default	Sample Rate
0–25	1–1
26–60	1–2
61–100	1–3
100–150	1–4
150+	1–10

The results of the sample determination process indicated that it would be necessary to obtain a sample of 50 per cent of the reporters in the mortgage company and commercial bank groups. Mutual savings banks were selected on a one for one basis. These reporters, however were merged with the National Association of Mutual Savings Banks sample which will be discussed later.

The actual firms chosen were selected at random and responses were excellent. Usable data were obtained from 36 of 38 savings banks, 41 of 51 commercial banks, and 105 of 129 mortgage companies. Because later checks revealed that mortgage companies had been under-sampled, the blow-up factor for that group had to be adjusted from 2.0 to 2.64.

QUESTIONNAIRE AND CODING INSTRUCTIONS

The Mortgage Bankers Association of America conducted a survey of the characteristics of delinquent mortgage loans, using data as of June 30, 1963. Table A3 lists the categories as they appeared on the questionnaire. Table A4 shows the format used in putting the data on punch cards.

National Association of Mutual Savings Banks Data

PARTICIPATING INSTITUTIONS

The savings banks included in the NAMSB survey were selected basically on a random basis. The original list was then modified in order to integrate it with that of the MBA so that the combined list would reflect more accurately the distribution of savings banks with respect to (1) geographical location (2) size (3) mortgage portfolio composition (FHA, VA, and conventional loans) and (4) the proportion of delinquent loans to total loans.

Each institution in the NAMSB survey was sent instruction sheet (1), (2), or (3), depending on the within-institution sampling rate requested. This provided for a 1-2, 1-3, or a 1-7 loan sample of delinquent loans. In each case the banks were asked to select a number of current loans equal to the number of delinquents reported on. The purpose of using different sampling ratios was to minimize the reporting burdens on the banks. Those having a larger number of delinquents selected a smaller proportion.

Altogether data were secured on about 1250 delinquent loans and an equal number of currents. This represents about 10 per cent of the total population of delinquents as of the survey date. In all, 73 banks participated in the survey (combined MBA and NAMSB).

INSTRUCTION SHEET: CHARACTERISTICS OF DELINQUENT MORTGAGE LOANS

Types of Loans Included.   Report only on current and delinquent loans in the 1- to 4-family property classification or the most closely corresponding property classification used by your institution. Include only loans on property located in your *own* state.

TABLE A 3

Characteristics of Delinquent Mortgage Loans:
Mortgage Bankers Association, June 30, 1963[a]

Your Loan Number
Type of Loan (check one)
　FHA
　VA
　Conventional
Status of Loan (check one)
　Delinquent 90 days or more
　In foreclosure
Currency
Service for:
　Life insurance company
　Savings bank
　Commercial bank
　　(code trust department 4)
　Trusteed funds
　FNMA
　Savings & loan association
　Own account
　Individuals & others
Description of Original Loan
　Date loan was closed
　Original selling price
　Original loan amount
　Term (mos.)

Interest Rate
　Contract rate
　Estimated yield to investor
Original Monthly Payment (including escrows)
Location (check one)
　Spot
　Tract
Property
　County location
　Age (yrs. or new)
Borrower—When Loan Was Closed
　Monthly Income
　　Primary
　　Secondary
　　Total
　Liquid Assets (excluding downpayment)
　Occupation
　　Professional or Technical
　　Proprietors or Managers
　　Clerical
　　Sales
　　Craftsmen & Foremen
　　Skilled Labor, manufacturing
　　Skilled Labor, non-manufacturing

Services
Laborer
Number of Dependents (Including wife)
Age of Family Head
Monthly Payments (including escrows)
Principal Balance (4-30-63)
Est. Current Value of Property
Marital Status (check one)
Married
Single
Current Value-to-Selling-Price ratio
Number of Prior Delinquencies That Were Cured
History of Loan
Apply to Current Delinquent Problem Only
Date of
First Unpaid Installment
First Contact
Number of Contacts
Letter
Phone
Personal
Reason For Delinquency
Death or illness in family
Family or marital problems

Over-obligated, same income
Reduction in secondary income
Cost of home ownership increased
Increases in other living costs
Property unsatisfactory
Increase in dependents
Entered military service
Unable to sell or rent
Improper regard for obligations
Property abandoned
Describe Nature and Term of Forbearance, if any (if necessary, explain on separate sheet and identify by loan number)
Date Placed in Foreclosure

aThe questionnaire used by the National Association of Mutual Savings Banks, dated December 31, 1963, is almost identical to this questionnaire. It differs in only three respects: (1) The question regarding the institution for which the loan was serviced was dropped; (2) The question regarding the nature and term of forebearance was dropped; and (3) Two additional employment categories were added – military and retired.

TABLE A 4

Punch Card Format, Characteristics of Delinquent Mortgage Loans[a]

Respondent Identification
  Region
  State
  City
  Type of business
Loan Identification
  Loan number
  Page
  Line
Type of Loan
  FHA, 203
  FHA, 221
  FHA, other
  VA
  Conventional
  Combination
  Not reported
Status of Loan
  90-day delinquent
  In foreclosure
  Current
  Not reported
Serviced for:
  Codes on form RD-3

Not reported
Description of Loan (compute age of
  mortgage as of 6/30/63
  June 30, 1958 and earlier
  July–December 1958
  January–June 1959
  July–December 1959
  January–June 1960
  July–December 1960
  January–June 1961
  July–December 1961
  January–June 1962
  July–December 1962
  January–June 1963
  Not reported
Original Selling Price
  Under $10,000
  $10,000–11,000
  $11,000–12,000
  $12,000–13,000
  $13,000–14,000
  $14,000–15,000
  $15,000–16,000
  $16,000–17,000

$17,000–18,000
$18,000–19,000
$19,000–20,000
$20,000 and over
Not reported
Original Loan Amount (compute loan to selling price ratio and code; compute principal balance to selling price ratio and code; compute principal balance to market value ratio and code)
Less than 75 per cent
75–80 per cent
80–85 per cent
85–90 per cent
90–95 per cent
95 per cent and over
Not reported
Terms (months) (convert to years and code)
Less than 240 months
240–300 months
300–360 months
360 months or more
Not reported
Contract Interest Rate (round to nearest .25 per cent)

4.00 per cent or less
4.25 per cent
4.50 per cent
4.75 per cent
5.00 per cent
5.25 per cent
5.50 per cent
5.75 per cent
6.00 per cent
6.25 per cent
6.50 per cent
7.00 per cent
More than 7.00 per cent
Not reported
Yield to Investor (same as contract interest rate; round to nearest .25 per cent)
Original Monthly Payment (include escrow)
Current Monthly Payment (include escrow)
Less than $70
$70–80
$80–90
$90–100
$100–110
$110–120

$120–140
$140–150
$150 and above

Type of Transaction
  Spot
  Tract
  Not reported

County (alphabetical within alphabetical listing of states, see Rand McNally)

Age
  New
  Less than 1 year
  1–2 years
  2–5 years
  5–10 years
  10 years and older
  Existing
  Not reported

Monthly Income
  Primary, original
  Primary, current
  Total, original
  Total, current
  Not reported

(compute ratio of monthly income to monthly payment and code)
  Less than 5 per cent
  5–10 per cent
  10–15 per cent
  15–20 per cent
  20–25 per cent
  25–30 per cent
  30–35 per cent
  35 per cent or more
  Not reported

Liquid Assets, Original
Liquid Assets, Current
(compute ratio of liquid asset to monthly payment)
  Less than 1 (or modest) (or small)
  1–2
  2–3
  3–4
  4–5
  5–10
  10 or more
  Not reported

Occupation, Original Borrower
Occupation, New Borrower
Marital Status, Original Borrower
Marital Status, New Borrower
  Married
  Single
  Divorced
  Widowed
  Separated
  Not reported
Number of Dependents (include wife)
  Original borrower
  New borrower
  Not reported
Age of Head of Family, Original Borrower
Age of Head of Family, New Borrower
  Less than 25 years
  25–30 years
  30–35 years
  35–40 years
  40–45 years
  45–50 years
  50–60 years
  60 years or more
  Not reported
Borrower
  Same
  New
  Not reported
Estimated Current Value of Property (compute ratio of current value to original selling price and code)
  100 per cent or more
  95–100 per cent
  90–95 per cent
  85–90 per cent
  80–85 per cent
  75–80 per cent
  Less than 75 per cent
  Not reported
Number of Prior Delinquencies
  Many, numerous or several
  Chronic
  Not reported
Date of First Default (compute period from June 30, 1963)
  May and June 1963

April 1963
March 1963
February 1963
July 1962 through January 1963
12–18 months
18 months or more
Not reported
Date of First Contact With Borrower (compute period from date of first default)
Less than 1 week
1–2 weeks
2–3 weeks
3–4 weeks
4–8 weeks
8–12 weeks
12 weeks or more
Not reported
Number of Contacts Made By Letter
Number of Contacts Made By Phone
Number of Personal Contacts
Constant
Several
Numerous
Many

Not reported
Reason for Delinquency of Forbearance (code on RD-3 form)
Not reported
Forbearance, Type or Nature of:
Satisfied or about to be; removed from foreclosure
Pending sale
Pending recovery from illness, imminent death, death
Pending receipt of other sources of income
Practiced forbearance, type undefined
Impossible to forbear
Repayment program
None
Not reported
Foreclosures (compute months in foreclosure status)
Not in foreclosure
June 1963
May 1963
April 1963
March 1963
February 1963
January 1963
Not reported

aCoded for a survey conducted by Mortgage Bankers Association of America, June 30, 1963.

Delinquent Loans. A sample of the delinquent loans reported by the bank as of December 31, 1963, in the NAMSB Quarterly Mortgage Delinquency Survey. This includes loans which are three or more payments overdue on a monthly program or one or more payments overdue on a quarterly program. Includes also all loans in the process of foreclosure as of December 31, 1963.

Current Loans. A sample of current loans held on December 31, 1963 equal to the number of delinquent loans, selected according to the procedures outlined below.

Selecting Samples of Current and Delinquent Loans

Note: To reduce the reporting burden, the following procedures were designed to *select a sample of loans*. To assure reliability, it is important that this procedure be followed without deviation.

1. On a separate worksheet, simply list the number and type of each 1- to 4-family loan that was reported as delinquent in the Mortgage Delinquency Survey on December 31, 1963 (FHA, VA, and conventional).
2. On this worksheet, place a check beside the first, fourth, and seventh loan, continuing to the end of the list, checking every third loan.[1]
3. Alongside each loan checked on the worksheet, enter the *next consecutive number* of a loan that is *current and of the same type* (see example below, as to breakdown by type of loan) as the delinquent loan or loan in foreclosure.

Loans Delinquent 90 Days or More or in Foreclosure		Current Loans	
Loan Number	Type of Loan	Loan Number	Type of Loan
8,543✔	FHA, 203b	8,544	FHA, 203b
10,782	VA		
9,543	Conventional		
12,492✔	VA	12,495[2]	VA
6,781	FHA, 203i		
392	FHA, 203b		
4,001✔	FHA, 203b	4,002	FHA, 203b

[1] The other two worksheets differ only in the sampling techniques (one asks that every other delinquent loan be checked; the other calls for every seventh delinquent loan).

[2] Intervening loans 12,493 and 12,494 are not VA.

4. Post the loan numbers of the delinquent loans and the loans in foreclosure that were checked, as well as all current loans listed to the first column of the reporting form provided.

Selected Definitions

1. *Type of Loan.*   Consider a combination FHA-VA loan as one loan and report as FHA.

2. *Borrower—When Present Delinquency Developed.*   Regardless of legal arrangement and liability under the mortgage contract, if a new borrower has, in effect, assumed responsibility for the mortgage prior to present delinquency, check "new" and supply as much of the indicated information as is available in your collection department.

3. *Primary and Secondary Income.*   Primary income is the total income of the head of the household as shown in your records. Secondary income is total income of other members of the household.

4. *Liquid Assets.*   Generally speaking, total amount of liquid assets (such as bank deposits, savings and loan share accounts, U.S. Savings Bonds) held by borrower, as shown in your records.

5. *County Location of Property.*   For areas where primary political subdivision is not a county, then enter designation of the equivalent political subdivision, such as a township.

Notes

1. Please answer all questions from current records. *Do not seek additional information beyond that already in your files.*

2. Answer each question; if data are not available, enter N.A.

3. Enter all information directly on the questionnaire and separate worksheet used to select sample of loans. Information may be written by hand.

Kindly send one copy of the completed forms and the worksheet list prepared to select the loans by Friday, February 21, 1964, if possible to: Research Department; National Association of Mutual Savings Banks; 200 Park Avenue, New York, N.Y. 10017.

Appendix B

Regression Equations and Values for Lorenz Curves

Explanation of Regression Tables

Tables B1 through B13 contain the output from the full regression equations. These cover delinquency risk (current vs. noncurrent) for all three samples, conditional foreclosure risk (delinquent vs. in foreclosure) for the same groups, and straight foreclosure risk (current vs. in foreclosure) for the USSLL sample. Delinquency and conditional foreclosure risk equations appear in both individual and pooled versions.

Over-all statistics are indicated at the top of each table. These include the constant term for each equation, coefficient of determination (R^2), standard error of the estimate (S_e), number of observations on which the equation is based (N), and over-all F ratio (FOR).

Headings above the columns indicate the mnemonic symbol used to designate each variable, the actual variable name, the partial regression coefficient (b), the standard error of the regression coefficient (S_b), the "t" value for each coefficient (b/S_b), the beta coefficient (β), and the partial correlation between the independent variable and the dependent (r_{yx}). A single asterisk (*) beside the "t" value of F ratio indicates that the statistic is significant at the 5 per cent level. A double asterisk (**) indicates significance at the 1 per cent level.

TABLE B 1

Regression–USSLL:
Current vs. Noncurrent
Constant: .063601   N: 6472
R^2 : .1148   FOR: 20.35**
S_e : .0117

Variable Symbol	Variable Name	b	S_b	b/S_b	β	r_{yx}
RLS	Loan/Value ratio	2.018 −1	4.281 −2	** 4.714 +0	6.962 −2	5.868 −2
T	Init. term to maturity	−1.065 −4	1.089 −4	−9.784 −1	−1.543 −2	−1.220 −2
RPI	Payment/Income ratio	−6.575 −2	9.920 −2	−6.629 −1	−8.491 −3	−8.266 −3
O_1	Self employed	6.892 −2	1.477 −2	** 4.666 +0	6.633 −2	5.809 −2
O_2	Executive or manager	−3.993 −2	1.708 −2	* −2.338 +0	−3.215 −2	−2.914 −2
O_3	Sales	7.139 −2	2.043 −2	** 3.494 +0	4.503 −2	4.353 −2
O_4	White collar	−8.378 −2	1.696 −2	** −4.939 +0	−6.643 −2	−6.147 −2
O_5	Unskilled labor	2.990 −2	1.895 −2	1.578 +0	2.055 −2	1.967 −2
O_6	Professional	−1.076 −1	4.588 −2	* −2.345 +0	−2.852 −2	−2.923 −2
O_7	Government service	−3.447 −2	4.437 −2	−7.769 −1	−9.387 −3	−9.687 −3
O_8	Other	−9.173 −3	2.384 −2	−3.847 −1	−4.971 −3	−4.797 −3
O_9	Skilled labor	0	0	0	0	0
DN_1	1 dependent(s)	2.692 −2	3.296 −2	8.167 −1	3.089 −2	7.018 −2
DN_2	2 "	5.034 −2	3.431 −2	1.467 +0	4.773 −2	1.829 −2
DN_3	3 "	8.160 −2	3.477 −2	* 2.347 +0	7.865 −2	2.926 −2
DN_4	4 "	9.510 −2	3.673 −2	** 2.587 +0	6.759 −2	3.225 −2
DN_5	5–6 "	1.210 −1	3.851 −2	** 3.142 +0	7.113 −2	3.915 −2
DN_6	7–8 "	2.365 −1	5.356 −2	** 4.416 +0	6.606 −2	5.499 −2
DN_7	9 or more "	−1.159 −3	8.010 −2	−1.447 −2	−1.862 −4	−1.804 −4
DN_8	No dependents	0	0	0	0	0

		Col1	Col2	Col3	Col4	Col5
SM_1	Married	-5.532 -2	3.560 -2	-1.554 +0	-3.360 -2	-1.938 -2
SM_2	Widowed	6.443 -2	4.197 -2	1.535 +0	2.447 -2	1.913 -2
SM_3	Divorced	5.174 -2	4.644 -2	1.114 +0	1.626 -2	1.389 -2
SM_4	Single	0	0	0	0	0
AB_1	Borrower age 30–34	-4.632 -2	1.789 -2	**-2.589 +0	-4.123 -2	-3.226 -2
AB_2	,, 35–39	-3.304 -2	1.761 -2	-1.876 +0	-3.097 -2	-2.338 -2
AB_3	,, 40–44	-6.048 -2	1.837 -2	**-3.293 +0	-5.272 -2	-4.103 -2
AB_4	,, 45–49	-8.170 -2	1.909 -2	**-4.280 +0	-6.796 -2	-5.330 -2
AB_5	,, 50–54	-5.091 -2	2.119 -2	*-2.402 +0	-3.600 -2	-2.994 -2
AB_6	,, 55–59	-6.509 -2	2.619 -2	*-2.485 +0	-3.461 -2	-3.097 -2
AB_7	,, 60 or over	-8.943 -2	2.883 -2	**-3.102 +0	-4.413 -2	-3.866 -2
AB_8	,, 20–29	0	0	0	0	0
P_1	Construction	6.049 -2	1.432 -2	** 4.223 +0	5.558 -2	5.258 -2
P_2	Repair	1.502 -1	2.458 -2	** 6.110 +0	7.795 -2	7.597 -2
P_3	Refinance	1.645 -1	1.337 -2	** 1.230 +1	1.718 -1	1.516 -1
P_4	Purchase	0	0	0	0	0
FJ_1	Jr. financing	1.611 -1	1.422 -2	** 1.133 +1	1.481 -1	1.399 -1
FJ_2	No jr. financing	0	0	0	0	0
R_1	Northeast	-1.211 -1	2.698 -2	**-4.488 +0	-6.249 -2	-5.588 -2
R_2	Mid-Atlantic	-1.146 -2	2.149 -3	**-5.333 +0	-8.919 -2	-6.636 -2
R_3	Southeast	1.534 -2	2.062 -2	7.438 -1	1.146 -2	9.275 -3
R_4	E. N. Central	4.079 -2	1.722 -2	* 2.369 +0	4.560 -2	2.953 -2
R_5	E. S. Central	2.916 -2	4.176 -2	6.983 -1	8.928 -3	8.708 -3
R_6	W. N. Central	1.147 -1	1.949 -2	** 5.885 +0	9.930 -2	7.319 -2
R_7	W. S. Central	4.896 -5	2.989 -2	1.638 -3	2.235 -5	2.042 -5
R_8	Mountain	-1.751 -1	4.844 -2	**-3.615 +0	-4.434 -2	-4.503 -2
R_9	Pacific	0	0	0	0	0

Note: All numbers within the body of the table are to be multiplied by 10 raised to the exponent indicated in the trailing digit of the number. Thus: $6.962\ -2 = 6.962\ (10)^{-2} = .06962$.

107

TABLE B 2

Regression—MBA:
Current vs. Noncurrent
Constant: .16665 8   N :3690
R^2 : .0381   FOR: 3.29**
S_e : .01624

Variable Symbol	Variable Name	b	S_b	b/S_b	β	r_{yx}
RLS	Loan/Value ratio	8.154 –1	1.323 –1	** 6.164 +0	1.513 –1	1.016 –1
T	Init. term to maturity	–3.652 –4	2.177 –4	–1.678 +0	–3.835 –2	–2.777 –2
RPI	Payment/Income ratio	–3.772 –1	1.891 –1	* –1.995 +0	–3.360 –2	–3.302 –2
O_1	Proprietor or manager	–7.971 –2	3.130 –2	* –2.547 +0	–4.907 –2	–4.215 –2
O_2	Salesman	2.157 –2	3.232 –2	6.673 –1	1.243 –2	1.105 –2
O_3	Clerical	–5.101 –2	3.824 –2	–1.334 +0	–2.384 –2	–2.209 –2
O_4	Unskilled laborer	3.358 –2	2.839 –2	1.183 +0	2.329 –2	1.959 –2
O_5	Professional or technical	–9.141 –2	2.724 –2	** –3.355 +0	–6.653 –2	–5.547 –2
O_6	Service	3.639 –3	2.819 –2	1.291 –1	2.505 –3	2.138 –3
O_7	Craftsman or foreman	–1.535 –2	3.291 –2	–4.664 –1	–8.656 –3	–7.724 –3
O_8	Skilled laborer	0	0	0	0	0
DN_1	1 dependent(s)	–2.061 –2	7.278 –2	–2.832 –1	–1.523 –2	–4.689 –3
DN_2	2 ,,	–2.360 –2	7.311 –2	–3.228 –1	–1.971 –2	–5.346 –3
DN_3	3 ,,	2.981 –3	7.364 –2	4.048 –2	2.677 –3	6.703 –4
DN_4	4 ,,	9.833 –2	7.495 –2	1.312 +0	7.614 –2	2.172 –2
DN_5	5 ,,	1.028 –1	7.847 –2	1.310 +0	5.466 –2	2.169 –2
DN_6	6 ,,	1.390 –1	9.145 –2	1.520 +0	4.064 –2	2.517 –2
DN_7	7 ,,	–4.586 –2	9.967 –2	–4.601 –1	–1.091 –2	–7.620 –3
DN_8	8 ,,	7.095 –2	1.263 –1	5.619 –1	1.121 –2	9.306 –3
DN_9	No dependents	0	0	0	0	0
SM_1	Married	–2.794 –2	5.871 –2	–4.759 –1	–1.162 –2	–7.881 –3
SM_2	Not married	0	0	0	0	0

AB_1	Borrower age 25–29	−2.307 −2	2.997 −2	−7.698 −1	−2.091 −2	−1.275 −2
AB_2	” 30–34	−1.059 −2	3.143 −2	−3.369 −1	−8.881 −3	−5.579 −3
AB_3	” 35–39	−9.180 −2	3.292 −2	**−2.789 +0	−7.022 −2	−4.613 −2
AB_4	” 40–44	−3.196 −2	3.761 −2	−8.498 −1	−1.876 −2	−1.407 −2
AB_5	” 45–49	−3.682 −2	4.335 −2	−8.494 −1	−1.686 −2	−1.407 −2
AB_6	” 50–59	−1.253 −1	5.312 −2	*−2.359 +0	−4.458 −2	−3.904 −2
AB_7	” 60 or over	−6.134 −2	7.399 −2	−8.290 −1	−1.455 −2	−1.373 −2
AB_8	” less than 25	0	0	0	0	0
R_1	Northeast	1.532 −2	3.564 −2	4.298 −1	9.224 −3	7.117 −3
R_2	Mid-Atlantic	0	0	0	0	0
R_3	Southeast	4.427 −3	3.109 −2	1.424 −1	3.421 −3	2.358 −3
R_4	E. N. Central	−2.133 −1	1.055 −1	*−2.021 +0	−3.378 −2	−3.345 −2
R_5	E. S. Central	1.471 −2	3.111 −2	4.729 −1	1.148 −2	7.832 −3
R_6	W. N. Central	8.410 −2	6.400 −2	1.314 +0	2.317 −2	2.175 −2
R_7	W. S. Central	4.562 −2	3.249 −2	1.404 +0	3.270 −2	2.325 −2
R_8	Mountain	3.003 −2	2.970 −2	1.011 +0	2.564 −2	1.674 −2
R_9	Pacific	0	0	0	0	0
TLD_1	LIC	−3.743 −2	8.142 −2	−4.597 −1	−3.411 −2	−7.613 −3
TLD_2	MSB	−2.598 −2	8.131 −2	−3.195 −1	−2.347 −2	−5.291 −3
TLD_3	CB	−1.787 −1	9.254 −1	−1.931 −1	−6.255 −3	−3.198 −3
TLD_4	Trusteed funds	−7.787 −1	8.920 −1	−8.730 −1	−3.149 −2	−1.446 −2
TLD_5	FNMA	−7.152 −3	8.194 −2	−8.728 −2	−5.602 −3	−1.445 −3
TLD_6	SLA	−2.877 −2	9.036 −2	−3.184 −1	−1.094 −2	−5.273 −3
TLD_7	Own	3.156 −2	8.436 −2	3.741 −1	1.971 −2	6.195 −3
TLD_8	Individual or other	0	0	0	0	0
TLN_1	FHA 203	−1.869 −1	5.584 −2	**−3.347 +0	−1.869 −1	−5.535 −2
TLN_2	VA	−2.355 −1	5.944 −2	**−3.962 +0	−2.327 −1	−6.547 −2
TLN_3	FHA other	−2.079 −1	7.552 −2	**−2.753 +0	−6.790 −2	−4.554 −2
TLN_4	Conventional	0	0	0	0	0

Notes: All numbers within the body of the table are to be multiplied by 10 raised to the exponent indicated in the trailing digit of the number. Thus: 6.962 −2 = 6.962 $(10)^{-2}$ = .06962.

TABLE B 3

Regression–NAMSB:
Current vs. Noncurrent

Constant: 1.273   N: 2419
R^2 : .0495   FOR: 3.77**
S_e : .01996

Variable Symbol	Variable Name	b	S_b	b/S_b	β	r_{yx}
RLS	Loan/Value ratio	5.423 −1	9.577 −2	** 5.663 +0	1.674 −1	8.351 −2
T	Init. term to maturity	−3.846 −4	1.725 −4	*−2.230 +0	−6.139 −2	−1.009 −2
RPI	Payment/income ratio	−1.568 −1	1.853 −1	−8.463 −1	−1.790 −2	−1.650 −3
O_1	Prop. or manager	3.386 −2	3.330 −2	1.017 +0	2.549 −2	1.929 −2
O_2	Salesman	1.149 −1	3.909 −2	** 2.940 +0	6.744 −2	6.440 −2
O_3	Clerical worker	3.834 −3	4.353 −2	8.808 −2	1.981 −3	−8.190 −3
O_4	Unskilled laborer	6.704 −2	3.846 −2	1.743 +0	4.082 −2	5.438 −2
O_5	Professional or tech.	−6.690 −2	3.569 −2	−1.874 +0	−4.455 −2	−7.504 −2
O_6	Service worker	1.644 −2	3.602 −2	4.565 −1	1.075 −2	−2.690 −3
O_7	Craftsman or foreman	−4.720 −3	4.248 −2	−1.111 −1	−2.500 −3	−1.040 −2
O_8	Military	−1.568 −1	1.215 −1	−1.290 +0	−2.624 −2	−2.615 −2
O_9	Retired	−6.186 −2	1.309 −1	−4.727 −1	−1.090 −2	−1.620 −2
O_{10}	Skilled labor	0	0	0	0	0
DN_1	1 dependent(s)	−4.563 −2	8.019 −2	−5.690 −1	−3.464 −2	−5.728 −2
DN_2	2 "	−5.240 −2	8.192 −2	−6.397 −1	−4.407 −2	−7.860 −2
DN_3	3 "	−5.140 −3	8.142 −2	−6.313 −2	−4.550 −3	−2.225 −2
DN_4	4 "	1.272 −1	8.262 −2	1.539 +0	9.721 −2	1.089 −1

DN_5	5　　"	1.141 −1	8.888 −2	1.284 +0	5.486 −2	4.899 −2
DN_6	6　　"	1.786 −1	1.007 −1	1.773 +0	5.666 −2	5.335 −2
DN_7	7　　"	1.089 −1	1.261 −1	8.638 −1	2.213 −2	2.353 −2
DN_8	8 or more dependents	−3.726 −2	1.331 −1	−2.800 −1	−7.030 −3	−1.374 −2
DN_9	No dependents	0	0	0	0	0
SM_1	Married	−3.738 −2	7.611 −2	−4.911 −1	−1.663 −2	2.000 −5
SM_2	Not married	0	0	0	0	0
AB_1	Borrower age 25—29	−4.199 −2	4.525 −2	−9.280 −1	−3.632 −2	−2.366 −2
AB_2	"　" 30—34	−4.250 −2	4.666 −2	−9.108 −1	−3.595 −2	4.830 −3
AB_3	"　" 35—39	−3.998 −2	4.815 −2	−8.303 −1	−3.156 −2	1.269 −1
AB_4	"　" 40—44	1.002 −2	5.246 −2	1.910 −1	6.420 −3	2.860 −2
AB_5	"　" 45—49	−5.111 −2	5.828 −2	−8.771 −1	−2.455 −2	−1.183 −2
AB_6	"　" 50—59	−4.918 −2	5.875 −2	−8.371 −1	−2.436 −2	−2.452 −2
AB_7	"　" 60 or over	9.509 −2	1.114 −1	8.537 −1	2.159 −2	−4.444 −3
AB_8	"　" less than 25	0	0	0	0	0
R_1	Northeast	−1.918 −2	1.639 −2	−1.170 −1	−1.909 −2	3.550 −3
R_2	Mid-Atlantic	−3.071 −2	1.649 −1	−1.863 −1	−3.061 −2	−3.460 −3
R_3	Southeast	−2.862 −2	2.260 −1	−1.266 −1	−3.680 −3	−3.200 −4
R_4	E. N. Central	0				
R_5	E. S. Central	0				
R_6	W. N. Central	0	No loans included in these regions.			
R_7	W. S. Central	0				
R_8	Mountain	0				
R_9	Pacific	0				
TLN_1	FHA	−6.737 −2	3.328 −2	*−2.024 +0	−6.193 −2	6.300 −4
TLN_2	VA	−7.635 −2	3.363 −2	*−2.270 +0	−7.456 −2	8.200 −4
TLN_3	Conventional	0	0	0	0	0

Note: All numbers within the body of the table are to be multiplied by 10 raised to the exponent indicated in the trailing digit of the number. Thus: 6.962 -2 = (6.962) (10)⁻² = .06962.

In this table r_{yx} is a simple correlation, not a partial as in the other appendix tables.

111

TABLE B 4

Regression (Pooled)—USSLL:
Current vs. Noncurrent

Constant: .284506 N: 6472
R^2 : .0807 FOR: 18.24**
S_e : .01195

Variable Symbol	Variable Name	b	S_b	b/S_b	β	r_{yx}
RLS	Loan/Value ratio	2.014 −1	4.324 −2	** 4.658 +0	6.948 −2	5.794 −2
T	Init. term to maturity	−4.285 −4	1.053 −4	**−4.070 +0	−6.208 −2	−5.064 −2
RPI	Payment/income ratio	−7.991 −2	1.006 −1	−7.944 −1	−1.032 −2	−9.898 −3
O_1	Prop., self employed	7.269 −2	1.497 −2	** 4.856 +0	6.996 −2	6.040 −2
O_2	Salesman	8.012 −2	2.074 −2	** 3.864 +0	5.054 −2	4.809 −2
O_3	Clerical	−9.977 −2	1.723 −2	**−5.790 +0	−7.911 −2	−7.195 −2
O_4	Unskilled laborer	3.828 −2	1.928 −2	* 1.986 +0	2.631 −2	0
O_5	Prof., exec. or tech.	−5.315 −2	1.693 −2	**−3.140 +0	−4.446 −2	−3.908 −2
O_6	Service or other	−9.670 −3	2.279 −2	−4.244 −1	−5.618 −3	−5.288 −3
O_7	Skilled laborer	0	0	0	0	0
DN_1	1 dependent(s)	5.147 −2	3.195 −2	1.611 +0	5.907 −2	2.007 −2
DN_2	2 ,,	7.013 −2	3.302 −2	* 2.124 +0	6.649 −2	2.645 −2
DN_3	3 ,,	1.090 −1	3.351 −2	** 3.253 +0	1.051 −1	4.051 −2
DN_4	4 ,,	1.170 −1	3.563 −2	** 3.284 +0	8.320 −2	4.089 −2
DN_5	5−6 ,,	1.549 −1	3.750 −2	** 4.131 +0	9.103 −2	5.141 −2
DN_6	7 or more dependents	1.995 −1	4.883 −2	** 4.086 +0	6.405 −2	5.085 −2
DN_7	No dependents	0	0	0	0	0
SM_1	Married	−9.910 −2	2.565 −2	**−3.864 +0	−6.502 −2	−4.809 −2
SM_2	Not married	0	0	0	0	0

AB_1	Borrower age 30–34	−3.786 −2	1.819 −2	*−2.082 +0	−3.370 −2	−2.594 −2
AB_2	" 35–39	−2.732 −2	1.786 −2	−1.530 +0	−2.561 −2	−1.905 −2
AB_3	" 40–44	−5.431 −2	1.859 −2	**−2.922 +0	−4.734 −2	−3.639 −2
AB_4	" 45–49	−6.755 −2	1.922 −2	***−3.515 +0	−5.619 −2	−4.375 −2
AB_5	" 50–59	−4.268 −2	1.922 −2	*−2.221 +0	−3.683 −2	−2.766 −2
AB_6	" 60 or more	−8.370 −2	2.875 −2	***−2.911 +0	−4.130 −2	−3.625 −2
AB_7	" 20–29	0	0	0	0	0
R_1	Northeast	−1.841 −1	2.681 −2	**−6.866 +0	−9.498 −2	−8.523 −2
R_2	Mid-Atlantic	−1.897 −1	2.074 −2	**−9.146 +0	−1.477 −1	−1.132 −1
R_3	Southeast	3.342 −3	2.067 −2	1.617 −1	2.496 −3	2.014 −3
R_4	E. N. Central	−9.508 −3	1.709 −2	−5.611 −1	−1.072 −2	−6.991 −3
R_5	E. S. Central	−2.039 −2	4.182 −2	−4.876 −1	−6.244 −3	−6.076 −3
R_6	W. N. Central	6.009 −2	1.943 −2	**3.093 +0	5.203 −2	3.851 −2
R_7	W. S. Central	−4.495 −2	3.015 −2	−1.491 +0	−2.052 −2	−1.858 −2
R_8	Mountain	−2.272 −1	4.911 −2	**−4.626 +0	−5.754 −2	−5.754 −2
R_9	Pacific	0	0	0	0	0
TLD_1	LIC					
TLD_2	MSB					
TLD_3	CB					
TLD_4	Trusteed funds					
TLD_5	FNMA		All 0 since $TLD=TLD_6$ and $TLN=TLN_3$			
TLD_6	SLA					
TLD_7	Own					
TLD_8	Indiv. and other					
TLN_1	FHA					
TLN_2	VA					
TLN_3	Conventional					

Note: All numbers within the body of the table are to be multiplied by 10 raised to the exponent indicated in the trailing digit of the number. Thus: 6.962 −2 = 6.962 $(10)^{-2}$ = .06962.

113

TABLE B 5

Regression (Pooled)–MBA:
Current vs. Noncurrent
Constant: .199882   N: 3690
R^2 : .0358   FOR: 3.48**
S_e : .01625

Variable Symbol	Variable Name	b	S_b	b/S_b	β	r_{yx}
RLS	Loan/Value ratio	6.715 −1	1.222 −1	** 5.495 +0	1.246 −1	9.056 −2
T	Init. term to maturity	−6.079 −4	2.044 −4	**−2.974 +0	−6.383 −2	−4.916 −2
RPI	Payment/Income ratio	−3.505 −1	1.892 −1	−1.852 +0	−3.122 −2	−3.063 −2
O_1	Propr., self-employed	−7.347 −2	2.983 −2	*−2.463 +0	−4.523 −2	−4.072 −2
O_2	Salesman	2.155 −2	3.097 −2	6.959 −1	1.243 −2	1.152 −2
O_3	Clerical	−4.577 −2	3.715 −2	−1.232 +0	−2.139 −2	−2.039 −2
O_4	Unskilled labor	3.531 −2	2.681 −2	1.317 +0	2.449 −2	2.179 −2
O_5	Prof., exec. or tech.	−8.486 −2	2.553 −2	**−3.324 +0	−6.176 −2	−5.493 −2
O_6	Service or other	5.919 −3	2.664 −2	2.222 −1	4.075 −3	3.678 −3
O_7	Skilled laborer	0	0	0	0	0
DN_1	1 dependent(s)	−5.737 −2	6.204 −2	−9.246 −1	−4.239 −2	−1.530 −2
DN_2	2 "	−6.416 −2	6.116 −2	−1.049 +0	−5.358 −2	−1.736 −2
DN_3	3 "	−3.923 −2	6.138 −2	−6.391 −1	−3.523 −2	−1.058 −2
DN_4	4 "	6.048 −2	6.280 −2	9.631 −1	4.683 −2	1.594 −2
DN_5	5−6 "	7.300 −2	6.505 −2	1.112 +0	4.348 −2	1.840 −2
DN_6	7 or more dependents	−5.121 −2	8.300 −2	−6.170 −1	−1.456 −2	−1.021 −2
DN_7	No dependents	0	0	0	0	0
SM_1	Married	2.407 −2	5.950 −2	4.045 −1	8.288 −3	6.693 −3
SM_2	Not married	0	0	0	0	0

AB_1	Borrower age 30–34	5.203 −3	2.205 −2	2.3 60 −1	4.365 −3	3.906 −3
AB_2	,, ,, 35–39	−7.156 −2	2.423 −2	**−2.953 +0	−5.474 −2	−4.881 −2
AB_3	,, ,, 40–44	−1.184 −2	3.038 −2	−3.897 −1	−6.950 −3	−6.449 −3
AB_4	,, ,, 45–49	−1.786 −2	3.797 −2	−4.704 −1	−8.177 −3	−7.785 −3
AB_5	,, ,, 50–59	−1.048 −1	4.879 −2	*−2.148 +0	−3.730 −2	−3.552 −2
AB_6	,, ,, 60 or over	−5.805 −2	7.145 −2	−8.125 −1	−1.377 −2	−1.345 −2
AB_7	,, ,, 20–29	0	0	0	0	0
R_1	Northeast	1.588 −2	3.561 −2	4.459 −1	9.564 −3	7.380 −3
R_2	Mid-Atlantic	0	0	0	0	0
R_3	Southeast	1.018 −2	3.107 −2	3.276 −1	7.866 −3	5.422 −3
R_4	E. N. Central	−2.157 −1	1.056 −1	*−2.042 +0	−3.415 −2	−3.378 −2
R_5	E. S. Central	2.155 −2	3.104 −2	6.942 −1	1.682 −2	1.149 −2
R_6	W. N. Central	8.418 −2	6.397 −2	1.316 +0	2.319 −2	2.178 −2
R_7	W. S. Central	4.663 −2	3.660 −2	1.274 +0	3.343 −2	2.109 −2
R_8	Mountain	6.763 −2	3.175 −2	*2.130 +0	5.775 −2	3.523 −2
R_9	Pacific	0	0	0	0	0
TLD_1	LIC	−7.265 −2	8.116 −2	−8.951 −1	−6.621 −2	−1.481 −2
TLD_2	MSB	−5.178 −2	8.122 −2	−6.375 −1	−4.677 −2	−1.055 −2
TLD_3	CB	−4.197 −2	9.249 −2	−4.538 −1	−1.462 −2	−7.510 −3
TLD_4	Trusteed funds	−1.035 −1	8.899 −2	−1.163 +0	−4.187 −2	−1.924 −2
TLD_5	FNMA	−3.491 −2	8.193 −2	−4.261 −1	−2.734 −2	−7.052 −3
TLD_6	SLA	−5.533 −2	9.023 −2	−6.132 −1	−2.104 −2	−1.015 −2
TLD_7	Own	1.261 −2	8.435 −2	1.495 −1	7.879 −3	2.475 −3
TLD_8	Indiv. or other	0	0	0	0	0
TLN_1	FHA	4.488 −3	3.859 −2	1.163 −1	2.582 −3	1.924 −3
TLN_2	VA	−6.547 −2	2.315 −2	**−2.828 +0	−6.425 −2	−4.675 −2
TLN_3	Conventional	0	0	0	0	0

Note: All numbers within the body of the table are to be multiplied by 10 raised to the exponent indicated in the trailing digit of the number. Thus: 6.962 -2 = 6.962 (10)-2 = .06962.

TABLE B 6

Regression (Pooled)—NAMSB:
Current vs. Noncurrent

Constant: .2060   N: 2419
R^2 : .04746 FOR: 4.41216**
S_e : .01996

Variable Symbol	Variable Name	b	S_b	b/S_b	β	r_{yx}
RLS	Loan/Value ratio	5.410×10^{-1}	9.454×10^{-2}	5.723×10^{0} **	1.670×10^{-1}	8.351×10^{-2}
T	Init. term to maturity	-3.903×10^{-4}	1.723×10^{-4}	-2.265×10^{0} *	-6.231×10^{-2}	-1.009×10^{-2}
RPI	Payment/Income ratio	-1.300×10^{-1}	1.848×10^{-1}	-7.037×10^{-1}	-1.484×10^{-2}	-1.650×10^{-3}
O_1	Propr. or self employed	3.507×10^{-2}	3.121×10^{-2}	1.124×10^{0}	2.640×10^{-2}	1.929×10^{-2}
O_2	Salesman	1.128×10^{-1}	3.742×10^{-2}	3.015×10^{0} **	6.624×10^{-2}	6.440×10^{-2}
O_3	Clerical worker	6.580×10^{-3}	4.204×10^{-2}	1.565×10^{-1}	3.400×10^{-3}	-8.190×10^{-3}
O_4	Unskilled worker	7.198×10^{-2}	3.674×10^{-2}	1.959×10^{0} *	4.383×10^{-2}	5.438×10^{-2}
O_5	Prof., exec. or tech.	-6.672×10^{-2}	3.383×10^{-2}	-1.999×10^{0} *	-4.503×10^{-2}	-7.504×10^{-2}
O_6	Service or other	3.030×10^{-3}	3.292×10^{-2}	9.204×10^{-2}	2.080×10^{-3}	1.310×10^{-2}
O_7	Skilled laborer	0	0	0	0	0
DN_1	1 dependent(s)	-1.044×10^{-1}	7.184×10^{-2}	-1.454×10^{0}	-7.928×10^{-2}	-5.728×10^{-2}
DN_2	2 "	-1.129×10^{-1}	7.191×10^{-2}	-1.571×10^{-2}	-9.498×10^{-2}	-7.860×10^{-2}
DN_3	3 "	-6.647×10^{-2}	7.170×10^{-2}	-9.271×10^{-1}	-5.884×10^{-2}	-2.225×10^{-2}
DN_4	4 "	6.407×10^{-2}	7.360×10^{-2}	8.704×10^{-1}	4.897×10^{-2}	1.089×10^{-1}
DN_5	5–6 "	7.139×10^{-2}	7.769×10^{-2}	9.189×10^{-1}	4.033×10^{-2}	7.166×10^{-2}
DN_6	7 or more dependents	-1.693×10^{-2}	1.012×10^{-1}	-1.673×10^{-1}	-4.670×10^{-3}	-7.930×10^{-3}
DN_7	No dependents	0	0	0	0	0
SM_1	Married	3.408×10^{-2}	7.134×10^{-2}	4.777×10^{-1}	1.379×10^{-2}	9.390×10^{-3}
SM_2	Not married	0	0	0	0	0

AB_1 Borrower age 30–34	-9.752 -3	2.810 -2	-3.471 -1	-8.250 -3	4.830 -3
AB_2 " " 35–39	-9.577 -3	3.028 -2	-3.163 -1	-7.560 -3	1.269 -2
AB_3 " " 40–44	4.169 -2	3.591 -2	1.161 +0	2.671 -2	2.860 -2
AB_4 " " 45–49	-1.507 -2	4.537 -2	-3.323 -1	-7.240 -3	-1.183 -2
AB_5 " " 50–59	-1.746 -2	4.571 -2	-3.821 -1	-8.650 -3	-2.452 -2
AB_6 " " 60 or over	1.039 -1	9.430 -2	1.101 +0	2.358 -2	-4.444 -3
AB_7 " " 20–29	0	0	0	0	0
R_1 Northeast	-2.463 -2	1.638 -1	-1.504 -1	-2.452 -2	-3.550 -3
R_2 Mid-Atlantic	-3.181 -2	1.647 -1	-1.931 -1	-3.171 -2	-3.460 -3
R_3 Southeast	2.901 -2	2.259 -1	1.284 -1	3.730 -3	3.200 -4
R_4 E. N. Central	0	0	0	0	0
R_5 E. S. Central	0	} No loans included in these regions.			
R_6 W. N. Central	0				
R_7 W. S. Central	0				
R_8 Mountain	0				
R_9 Pacific	0				
TLD_1 LIC	0				
TLD_2 MSB	0	} All loans made and held by MSB's.			
TLD_3 CB	0				
TLD_4 Trusteed funds	0				
TLD_5 FNMA	0				
TLD_6 SLA	0				
TLD_7 Own	0				
TLD_8 Individual or other	0				
TLN_1 FHA	-6.862 -2	3.323 -2	*-2.065 +0	-6.310 -2	6.300 -4
TLN_2 VA	-7.792 -2	3.340 -2	*-2.333 +0	-7.610 -2	8.300 -4
TLN_3 Conventional	0	0	0	0	0

Note: All numbers within the body of the table are to be multiplied by 10 raised to the exponent indicated in the trailing digit of the number. Thus: $6.962\text{-}2 = (6.962)(10)^{-2} = .06962$. In this table r_{yx} is a simple correlation, not a partial as in the other appendix tables.

117

TABLE B 7

Regression—USSLL:
Delinquent vs. Foreclosures

Constant: .013852   N: 1570
R^2 : .1299   FOR: 5.57**
S_e : .02385

Variable Symbol	Variable Name	b	S_b	b/S_b	β	r_{yx}
RLS	Loan/Value ratio	1.598 −2	5.410 −2	2.954 −1	9.423 −3	7.556 −3
T	Init. term to maturity	3.400 −4	1.383 −4	2.459 +0 *	8.414 −2	6.276 −2
RPI	Payment/Income ratio	2.705 −1	1.196 −1	2.262 +0 *	5.968 −2	5.775 −2
O_1	Self-employed	−1.255 −2	1.722 −2	−7.288 −1	−2.221 −2	−1.863 −2
O_2	Executive or manager	5.774 −2	2.460 −2	2.347 +0 *	6.830 −2	5.990 −2
O_3	Sales	3.232 −2	2.214 −2	1.460 +0	3.985 −2	3.732 −2
O_4	White collar	4.372 −3	2.632 −2	1.661 −1	4.383 −3	4.248 −3
O_5	Unskilled labor	−1.981 −2	2.220 −2	−8.922 −1	−2.429 −2	−2.281 −2
O_6	Professional	5.978 −4	1.072 −1	5.576 −3	1.351 −4	1.426 −4
O_7	Government service	9.607 −2	5.493 −2	1.749 +0	4.352 −2	4.468 −2
O_8	Other	3.142 −2	2.939 −2	1.069 +0	2.890 −2	2.734 −2
O_9	Skilled labor	0	0	0	0	0
DN_1	1 dependent(s)	6.775 −2	4.656 −2	1.455 +0	1.241 −1	3.720 −2
DN_2	2 "	1.860 −2	4.766 −2	3.903 −1	2.680 −2	9.981 −3
DN_3	3 "	3.325 −2	4.870 −2	6.828 −1	5.382 −2	1.746 −2
DN_4	4 "	3.588 −2	5.075 −2	7.070 −1	4.400 −2	1.808 −2
DN_5	5–6 "	−6.744 −3	5.132 −2	−1.314 −1	−7.422 −3	−3.360 −3
DN_6	7–8 "	−1.304 −2	6.122 −2	−2.130 −1	−8.001 −3	−5.446 −3
DN_7	9 or more dependents	4.569 −3	1.086 −2	4.207 −2	1.120 −3	1.076 −3
DN_8	No dependents	0	0	0	0	0

118

SM_1	Married	-6.072 -2	4.889 -2	-1.242 +0	-7.052 -2	-3.173 -2
SM_2	Widowed	-4.351 -2	5.049 -2	-8.617 -1	-3.288 -2	-2.203 -2
SM_3	Divorced	-4.504 -2	5.693 -2	-7.912 -1	-2.624 -2	-2.023 -2
SM_4	Single	0	0	0	0	0
AB_1	Borrower age 30–34	-2.608 -2	2.197 -2	-1.187 +0	-3.811 -2	-3.033 -2
AB_2	,, ,, 35–39	-1.005 -2	2.134 -2	-4.704 -1	-1.617 -2	-1.203 -2
AB_3	,, ,, 40–44	-3.025 -3	2.307 -2	-1.311 -1	-4.239 -3	-3.353 -3
AB_4	,, ,, 45–49	1.016 -2	2.484 -2	4.090 -1	1.295 -2	1.046 -2
AB_5	,, ,, 50–54	-1.983 -3	2.658 -2	-7.461 -2	-2.250 -3	-1.908 -3
AB_6	,, ,, 55–59	-7.205 -2	3.367 -2	-2.140 +0	-6.250 -2	-5.466 -2
AB_7	,, ,, 60 or over	-3.489 -2	3.844 -2	-9.076 -1	-2.578 -2	-2.320 -2
AB_8	,, ,, 20–29	0	0	0	0	0
P_1	Construction	7.191 -2	2.019 -2	** 3.561 +0	1.046 -1	9.069 -2
P_2	Repair	3.648 -2	3.005 -2	1.214 +0	3.359 -2	3.104 -2
P_3	Refinance	3.563 -2	1.661 -2	* 2.145 +0	6.782 -2	5.477 -2
P_4	Purchase	0	0	0	0	0
FJ_1	Jr. financing	5.644 -2	1.469 -2	** 3.841 +0	1.076 -1	9.776 -2
FJ_2	No jr. financing	0	0	0	0	0
R_1	Northeast	2.366 -1	5.092 -2	** 4.646 +0	1.203 -1	1.180 -1
R_2	Mid-Atlantic	-9.105 -2	4.180 -2	*-2.178 +0	-5.934 -2	-5.561 -2
R_3	Southeast	-6.781 -2	2.335 -2	**-2.904 +0	-9.572 -2	-7.405 -2
R_4	E. N. Central	-9.386 -2	1.957 -2	**-4.797 +0	-1.836 -1	-1.218 -1
R_5	E. S. Central	-1.272 -1	4.787 -2	***-2.657 +0	-6.948 -2	-6.779 -2
R_6	W. N. Central	-1.539 -1	2.273 -2	***-6.770 +0	-2.590 -1	-1.706 -1
R_7	W. S. Central	-8.009 -2	3.513 -2	*-2.280 +0	-6.497 -2	-5.822 -2
R_8	Mountain	-1.707 -1	2.219 -1	-7.693 -1	-1.859 -2	-1.967 -2
R_9	Pacific	0	0	0	0	0

Note: All numbers within the body of the table are to be multiplied by 10 raised to the exponent indicated in the trailing digit of the number. Thus: 6.962 -2 = 6.962 (10)⁻² = .06962.

119

TABLE B 8

Regression—MBA:
Delinquent vs. Foreclosures

Constant: .072275 N: 1817
R^2 : .0667 FOR: 5.92**
S_e : .0160

Variable Symbol	Variable Name	b	S_b	b/S_b		β	r_{yx}
RLS	Loan/Value ratio	4.773 −1	1.446 −1	3.300 +0	**	8.050 −2	5.457 −2
T	Init. term to maturity	3.920 −4	2.184 −4	1.795 +0		4.151 −2	2.971 −2
RPI	Payment/Income ratio	1.164 −1	1.914 −1	6.080 −1		1.016 −2	1.007 −2
O_1	Proprietor or manager	5.252 −2	3.212 −2	1.635 +0		3.067 −2	2.707 −2
O_2	Salesman	−8.986 −2	3.118 −2	−2.882 +0	**	−5.336 −2	−4.767 −2
O_3	Clerical	−3.464 −2	3.918 −2	−8.841 −1		−1.568 −2	−1.464 −2
O_4	Unskilled laborer	4.258 −2	2.707 −2	1.573 +0		3.069 −2	2.604 −2
O_5	Professional	−4.140 −2	2.809 −2	−1.474 +0		−2.823 −2	−2.440 −2
O_6	Service	1.165 −2	2.721 −2	4.282 −1		8.202 −3	7.091 −3
O_7	Craftsman or foreman	5.064 −2	3.263 −2	1.552 +0		2.854 −2	2.570 −2
O_8	Skilled laborer	0	0	0		0	0
DN_1	1 dependent(s)	8.542 −2	7.166 −2	1.192 +0		6.102 −2	1.974 −2
DN_2	2 ″	1.574 −2	7.096 −2	2.218 −1		1.276 −2	3.673 −3
DN_3	3 ″	−2.697 −3	7.223 −2	−3.734 −2		−2.388 −3	−6.184 −4
DN_4	4 ″	1.173 −2	7.304 −2	1.606 −2		9.579 −3	2.659 −3
DN_5	5 ″	5.175 −2	7.645 −2	6.769 −1		2.938 −2	1.121 −2
DN_6	6 ″	−6.819 −2	8.728 −2	−7.813 −1		−2.184 −2	−1.294 −2
DN_7	7 ″	7.839 −4	1.006 −1	7.796 −3		1.765 −4	1.291 −4
DN_8	8 ″	3.845 −1	1.243 −1	3.093 +0	**	6.141 −2	5.115 −2
DN_9	No dependents	0	0	0		0	0

SM_1	Married	2.765 −3	5.757 −2	4.803 −2	1.145 −3	7.954 −4
SM_2	Not married	0	0	0	0	0
AB_1	Borrower age 25−29	−2.208 −3	2.905 −2	−7.600 −2	−2.008 −3	−1.259 −3
AB_2	,, ,, 30−34	−3.233 −2	3.039 −2	−1.064 +0	−2.757 −2	−1.762 −2
AB_3	,, ,, 35−39	3.267 −4	3.267 −2	1.000 −2	2.402 −4	1.657 −4
AB_4	,, ,, 40−44	−6.213 −2	3.655 −2	−1.700 +0	−3.678 −2	−2.814 −2
AB_5	,, ,, 45−49	−6.388 −2	4.250 −2	−1.503 +0	−2.923 −2	−2.489 −2
AB_6	,, ,, 50−59	−5.040 −2	5.704 −2	−8.835 −1	−1.627 −2	−1.463 −2
AB_7	,, ,, 60 or over	−3.710 −1	7.623 −2	**−4.867 +0	−8.446 −2	−8.034 −2
AB_8	,, ,, less than 25	0	0	0	0	0
R_1	Northeast	−1.319 −1	3.585 −2	**−3.679 +0	−7.901 −2	−6.081 −2
R_2	Mid-Atlantic	0	0	0	0	0
R_3	Southeast	−5.280 −2	3.147 −2	−1.678 +0	−4.047 −2	−2.778 −2
R_4	E. N. Central	−2.681 −1	1.329 −1	*−2.017 +0	−3.306 −2	−3.339 −2
R_5	E. S. Central	−1.580 −2	3.110 −2	−5.081 −1	−1.229 −2	−8.415 −3
R_6	W. N. Central	−4.315 −2	6.118 −2	−7.053 −1	−1.252 −2	−1.168 −2
R_7	W. S. Central	5.244 −2	3.211 −2	1.633 +0	3.860 −2	2.703 −2
R_8	Mountain	−3.767 −2	2.987 −2	−1.261 +0	−3.232 −2	−2.088 −2
R_9	Pacific	0	0	0	0	0
TLD_1	LIC	3.888 −1	7.649 −2	** 5.083 +0	3.486 −1	8.388 −2
TLD_2	MSB	2.431 −1	7.657 −2	** 3.175 +0	2.196 −1	5.250 −2
TLD_3	CB	1.439 −1	8.855 −2	1.625 +0	4.948 −2	2.691 −2
TLD_4	Trusteed funds	3.677 −1	8.577 −2	** 4.287 +0	1.400 −1	7.083 −2
TLD_5	FNMA	3.154 −1	7.702 −2	** 4.095 +0	2.543 −1	6.766 −2
TLD_6	SLA	3.051 −1	8.597 −2	** 3.549 +0	1.146 −1	5.867 −2
TLD_7	Own	1.892 −1	7.983 −2	* 2.370 +0	1.207 −1	3.922 −2
TLD_8	Indiv. or other	0	0	0	0	0
TLN_1	FHA 203	−2.988 −1	5.582 −2	**−5.353 +0	−2.988 −1	−8.830 −2
TLN_2	VA	−3.335 −1	5.950 −2	**−5.605 +0	−3.293 −1	−9.242 −2
TLN_3	FHA other	−2.086 −1	7.509 −2	***−2.778 +0	−6.888 −2	−4.596 −2
TLN_4	Conventional	0	0	0	0	0

Note: All numbers within the body of the table are to be multiplied by 10 raised to the exponent indicated in the trailing digit of the number. Thus: $6.962 \ −2 = 6.962 \ (10)^{−2} = .06962$.

TABLE B 9

Regression—NAMSB:
Delinquent vs. Foreclosures
Constant: −.3646   N: 1215
R^2 : .10043   FOR: 3.99566**
S_e : .02760

Variable Symbol	Variable Name	b	S_b	b/S_b	β	r_{yx}
RLS	Loan/Value ratio	3.338 −1	1.223 −1	** 2.729 +0	1.156 −1	1.423 −1
T	Init. term to maturity	3.661 −4	2.062 −4	1.776 +0	6.868 −2	1.416 −1
RPI	Payment/Income ratio	−3.710 −1	2.186 −1	−1.697 +0	−4.999 −2	−2.570 −2
O_1	Propr. or manager	−3.717 −2	3.977 −2	−9.347 −1	−3.347 −2	1.980 −3
O_2	Salesman	−1.083 −1	4.403 −2	* −2.460 +0	−8.104 −2	−3.916 −2
O_3	Clerical worker	−9.470 −3	5.293 −2	−1.789 −1	−5.680 −3	1.945 −2
O_4	Unskilled laborer	2.563 −2	4.389 −2	5.839 −1	1.959 −2	1.143 −2
O_5	Professional or tech.	−6.235 −2	4.564 −2	−1.366 +0	−4.444 −2	−3.112 −2
O_6	Service worker	−2.477 −4	4.273 −2	−5.798 −3	−1.900 −4	−3.185 −2
O_7	Craftsman or foreman	−8.170 −2	5.131 −2	−1.592 +0	−5.008 −2	−4.324 −2
O_8	Military	−1.128 −1	1.713 −1	−6.582 −1	−1.849 −2	−8.030 −3
O_9	Retired	−6.397 −2	1.691 −1	−3.784 −1	−1.201 −2	−4.463 −2
O_{10}	Skilled laborer	0	0	0	0	0
DN_1	1 dependent(s)	3.570 −2	8.608 −2	4.148 −1	3.000 −2	2.145 −2
DN_2	2 ,,	5.483 −2	8.834 −2	6.207 −1	5.087 −2	5.280 −3
DN_3	3 ,,	4.954 −2	8.773 −2	5.647 −1	5.059 −2	1.134 −3

DN_4	7.546 −2	8.905 −2	8.474 −1	7.290 −2	3.732 −2
DN_5	1.902 −2	9.590 −2	1.983 −1	1.158 −2	−3.260 −2
DN_6	−1.776 −1	1.075 −1	−1.652 +0	−7.547 −2	−8.580 −2
DN_7	−4.106 −2	1.352 −1	−3.036 −1	−1.078 −2	−3.106 −2
DN_8 8 or more dependents	9.077 −1	3.753 −1	* 2.418 +0	7.915 −1	6.164 −2
DN_9 No dependents	0	0	0	0	0
SM_1 Married	−1.541 −1	7.966 −2	−1.934 +0	−8.106 −2	−7.689 −2
SM_2 Not married	0	0	0	0	0
AB_1 Borrower age 25−29	1.144 −1	5.108 −2	* 2.240 +0	1.144 −1	4.568 −2
AB_2 ,, ,, 30−34	8.814 −2	5.221 −2	1.688 +0	8.769 −2	−2.594 −2
AB_3 ,, ,, 35−39	7.864 −2	5.406 −2	1.455 +0	7.348 −2	−2.439 −2
AB_4 ,, ,, 40−44	1.874 −1	5.745 −2	** 3.262 +0	1.454 −1	6.182 −2
AB_5 ,, ,, 45−49	7.638 −2	6.792 −2	1.125 +0	4.206 −2	−3.364 −2
AB_6 ,, ,, 50−59	1.479 −1	6.946 −2	* 2.130 +0	8.209 −2	−6.960 −3
AB_7 ,, ,, 60 or over	1.404 −1	1.310 −1	1.072 +0	3.665 −2	−4.959 −2
AB_8 ,, ,, less than 25	0	0	0	0	0
R_1 Northeast	6.706 −2	1.964 −1	3.414 −1	7.749 −2	−1.907 −1
R_2 Mid-Atlantic	1.982 −1	1.980 −1	1.001 +0	2.294 −1	1.868 −1
R_3 Southeast	5.088 −2	2.751 −2	1.874 +0	7.575 −2	6.287 −2
R_4 E. N. Central	0				
R_5 E. S. Central	0				
R_6 W. N. Central	0	No loans included in these regions.		0	0
R_7 W. S. Central	0				
R_8 Mountain	0				
R_9 Pacific	0				
TLN_1 FHA	3.663 −2	3.930 −2	9.321 −1	3.910 −2	1.301 −1
TLN_2 VA	−6.772 −2	4.084 −2	−1.658 +0	−7.678 −2	−1.035 −2
TLN_3 Conventional	0	0	0	0	0

Note: All numbers within the body of the table are to be multiplied by 10 raised to the exponent indicated in the trailing digit of the number. Thus: $6.962 \ −2 = (6.962) (10)^{−2} = .06962$.

In this table r_{yx} is a simple correlation, not a partial as in the other appendix tables.

TABLE B 10

Regression (Pooled)–USSLL:
Delinquent vs. Foreclosures

Constant: .033297   N: 1570
R^2 : .1112   FOR: 6.211**
S_e : .02403

Variable Symbol	Variable Name	b	S_b	b/S_b	β	r_{yx}
RLS	Loan/Value ratio	4.914 −3	5.365 −2	9.160 −2	2.898 −3	2.335 −3
T	Init. term to maturity	4.106 −3	1.313 −4	** 3.127 +0	1.016 −1	7.946 −2
RPI	Payment/Income ratio	2.335 −1	1.192 −1	* 1.958 +0	5.151 −2	4.984 −2
O_1	Prop., self employed	−1.112 −2	1.715 −2	−6.484 −1	−1.968 −2	−1.652 −2
O_2	Salesman	3.003 −2	2.221 −2	1.352 +0	3.702 −2	3.444 −2
O_3	Clerical	7.238 −3	2.644 −2	2.738 −1	7.256 −3	6.980 −3
O_4	Unskilled laborer	−2.050 −2	2.230 −2	−9.192 −1	−2.514 −2	−2.343 −2
O_5	Prof., exec. or tec.	5.217 −2	2.423 −2	* 2.153 +0	5.864 −2	5.479 −2
O_6	Service or other	4.999 −2	2.672 −2	1.871 +0	5.067 −2	4.763 −2
O_7	Skilled laborer	0	0	0	0	0
DN_1	1 dependent(s)	5.956 −2	4.270 −2	1.395 +0	1.091 −1	3.554 −2
DN_2	2 ''	2.534 −3	4.339 −2	5.840 −2	3.650 −3	1.489 −3
DN_3	3 ''	1.743 −2	4.454 −2	3.913 −1	2.822 −2	9.974 −3
DN_4	4 ''	1.621 −2	4.682 −2	3.462 −1	1.988 −2	8.826 −3
DN_5	5–6 ''	−2.364 −2	4.749 −2	−4.978 −1	−2.602 −2	−1.269 −2
DN_6	7 or more dependents	−3.620 −2	5.646 −2	−6.412 −1	−2.384 −2	−1.634 −2
DN_7	No dependents	0	0	0	0	0
SM_1	Married	−1.593 −2	3.023 −2	−5.270 −1	−1.850 −2	−1.343 −2
SM_2	Not married	0	0	0	0	0

AB_1	Borrower age 30—34	-2.263 -2	2.191 -2	-1.033 +0	-3.307 -2	-2.633 -2
AB_2	,, ,, 35—39	-9.311 -3	2.114 -2	-4.405 -1	-1.498 -2	-1.123 -2
AB_3	,, ,, 40—44	-7.215 -4	2.280 -2	-3.165 -2	-1.011 -3	-8.067 -3
AB_4	,, ,, 45—49	1.270 -2	2.452 -2	5.179 -1	1.618 -2	1.320 -2
AB_5	,, ,, 50—59	-2.951 -2	2.351 -2	-1.255 +0	-4.060 -2	-3.198 -2
AB_6	,, ,, 60 or over	-4.075 -2	3.766 -2	-1.082 +0	-3.011 -2	-2.757 -2
AB_7	,, ,, 20—29	0	0	0	0	0
R_1	Northeast	2.112 -1	5.084 -2	** 4.154 +0	1.074 -1	1.053 -1
R_2	Mid-Atlantic	-1.015 -1	4.050 -2	*** -2.728 +0	-7.203 -2	-6.938 -2
R_3	Southeast	-4.907 -2	2.262 -2	* -2.169 +0	-6.926 -2	-5.520 -2
R_4	E. N. Central	-1.133 -1	1.923 -2	*** -5.891 +0	-2.217 -1	-1.485 -1
R_5	E. S. Central	-1.358 -1	4.753 -2	*** -2.857 +0	-7.416 -2	-7.265 -2
R_6	W. N. Central	-1.795 -1	2.203 -2	*** -8.149 +0	-3.020 -1	-2.034 -1
R_7	W. S. Central	-9.510 -2	3.491 -2	*** -2.724 +0	-7.714 -2	-6.926 -2
R_8	Mountain	-1.983 -1	2.225 -1	-8.913 -1	-2.160 -2	-2.271 -2
R_9	Pacific	0	0	0	0	0
TLD_1	LIC					
TLD_2	MSB					
TLD_3	CB					
TLD_4	Trusteed funds					
TLD_5	FNMA		All 0 since $TLD=TLD_6$ and $TLN=TLN_3$.			
TLD_6	SLA					
TLD_7	Own					
TLD_8	Indiv. and other					
TLN_1	FHA					
TLN_2	VA					
TLN_3	Conventional					

Note: All numbers within the body of the table are to be multiplied by 10 raised to the exponent indicated in the trailing digit of the number. Thus: $6.962\ \text{-}2 = 6.962\ (10)^{-2} = .06962$

TABLE B 11

Regression (Pooled)–MBA:
Delinquent vs. Foreclosures
Constant: .197605   N: 1817
R^2 : .0559   *FOR: 2.70**
S_e : .02304

Variable Symbol	Variable Name	b	S_b	b/S_b	β	r_{yx}
RLS	Loan/Value ratio	1.369 −1	1.925 −1	7.110 −1	2.309 −2	1.686 −2
T	Init. term to maturity	4.442 −5	2.930 −4	1.516 −1	4.703 −3	3.595 −3
RPI	Payment/Income ratio	1.139 −1	2.746 −1	4.148 −1	9.947 −3	9.836 −3
O_1	Prop., self employed	5.245 −2	4.437 −2	1.182 +0	3.063 −2	2.803 −2
O_2	Salesman	−9.566 −2	4.297 −2	*−2.226 +0	−5.680 −2	−5.271 −2
O_3	Clerical	−4.682 −2	5.494 −2	−8.522 −1	−2.113 −2	−2.021 −2
O_4	Unskilled labor	2.443 −2	3.684 −2	6.631 −1	1.761 −2	1.572 −2
O_5	Prof., exec. or tech.	−5.639 −2	3.808 −2	−1.481 +0	−3.845 −2	−3.509 −2
O_6	Service or other	1.931 −3	3.706 −2	5.210 −2	1.359 −3	1.236 −3
O_7	Skilled laborer	0	0	0	0	0
DN_1	1 dependent(s)	1.579 −1	8.508 −2	1.856 +0	1.128 −1	4.397 −2
DN_2	2 ,,	8.271 −2	8.340 −2	9.917 −1	6.707 −2	2.351 −2
DN_3	3 ,,	6.947 −2	8.399 −2	8.271 −1	6.150 −2	1.961 −2
DN_4	4 ,,	9.395 −2	8.518 −2	1.103 +0	7.671 −2	2.615 −2
DN_5	5–6 ,,	1.045 −1	8.932 −2	1.170 +0	6.659 −1	2.773 −2
DN_6	7 or more dependents	2.045 −1	1.177 −1	1.737 +0	5.620 −2	4.117 −2
DN_7	No dependents	0	0	0	0	0
SM_1	Married	−1.622 −1	8.444 −2	−1.921 +0	−5.281 −2	−4.550 −2
SM_2	Not married	0	0	0	0	0

	Col 1	Col 2	Col 3	Col 4	Col 5
AB_1 Borrower age 30–34	-3.185 -2	3.095 -2	-1.029 +0	-2.716 -2	-2.438 -2
AB_2 ,, ,, 35–39	1.541 -3	3.558 -2	4.331 -2	1.133 -3	1.027 -3
AB_3 ,, ,, 40–44	-6.669 -2	4.261 -2	-1.565 +0	-3.948 -2	-3.708 -2
AB_4 ,, ,, 45–49	-4.572 -2	5.400 -2	-8.466 -1	-2.092 -2	-2.007 -2
AB_5 ,, ,, 50–59	-7.933 -3	7.635 -2	-1.039 -1	-2.561 -3	-2.465 -3
AB_6 ,, ,, 60 or over	-3.919 -1	1.066 -1	**-3.676 +0	-8.922 -2	-8.684 -2
AB_7 ,, ,, 20–29	0	0	0	0	0
R_1 Northeast	-1.238 -1	5.152 -2	*-2.403 +0	-7.414 -2	-5.600 -2
R_2 Mid-Atlantic	0	0	0	0	0
R_3 Southeast	-4.859 -2	4.528 -2	-1.073 +0	-3.724 -2	-2.543 -2
R_4 E. N. Central	-2.640 -1	1.912 -1	-1.381 +0	-3.255 -2	-3.272 -2
R_5 E. S. Central	-1.290 -2	4.471 -2	-2.885 -1	-1.003 -2	-6.842 -3
R_6 W. N. Central	-5.256 -2	8.800 -2	-5.973 -1	-1.525 -2	-1.416 -2
R_7 W. S. Central	3.428 -2	5.220 -2	6.567 -1	2.523 -2	1.557 -2
R_8 Mountain	-2.828 -1	3.672 -1	-7.702 -1	-3.013 -2	-1.826 -2
R_9 Pacific	0	0	0	0	0
TLD_1 LIC	3.526 -1	1.093 -1	** 3.225 +0	3.161 -1	7.626 -2
TLD_2 MSB	2.056 -1	1.092 -1	1.882 +0	1.867 -1	4.459 -2
TLD_3 CB	1.105 -1	1.269 -1	8.709 -1	3.801 -2	2.065 -2
TLD_4 Trusteed funds	3.433 -1	1.227 -1	*** 2.799 +0	1.307 -1	6.624 -2
TLD_5 FNMA	2.828 -1	1.105 -1	* 2.560 +0	2.280 -1	6.061 -2
TLD_6 SLA	2.655 -1	1.231 -1	* 2.156 +0	9.974 -2	5.107 -2
TLD_7 Own	1.652 -1	1.146 -2	1.441 +0	1.054 -1	3.416 -2
TLD_8 Indiv. or other	0	0	0	0	0
TLN_1 FHA	4.884 -2	5.449 -2	8.963 -1	2.931 -2	2.125 -2
TLN_2 VA	-4.078 -3	3.324 -2	-1.227 -1	-4.004 -3	-2.911 -3
TLN_3 Conventional	0	0	0	0	0

Note: All numbers within the body of the table are to be multiplied by 10 raised to the exponent indicated in the trailing digit of the number. Thus: $6.962\ -2 = 6.962\ (10)^{-2} = .06962$.

127

TABLE B12

Regression (Pooled)–NAMSB:
Delinquent vs. Foreclosures
Constant: −.09709   N: 1215
R^2 : .0829   *FOR: 3.9418**
S_e : .0278l

Variable Symbol	Variable Name	b	S_b	b/S_b	β	r_{yx}
RLS	Loan/Value ratio	3.090 −1	1.213 −1	* 2.547 +0	1.070 −1	1.423 −1
T	Init. term to maturity	3.506 −4	2.074 −4	1.690 +0	6.576 −2	1.416 −1
RPI	Payment/Income ratio	−3.259 −1	2.196 −1	−1.484 +0	−4.392 −2	−2.570 −2
O_1	Prop. or self employed	−8.285 −3	3.840 −2	−2.157 −1	−7.460 −3	1.980 −3
O_2	Salesman	−8.333 −2	4.245 −2	*−1.963 +0	−6.234 −2	−3.916 −2
O_3	Clerical worker	1.112 −2	5.182 −2	2.146 −1	6.670 −3	1.945 −2
O_4	Unskilled laborer	3.521 −2	4.214 −2	8.355 −1	2.691 −2	1.143 −2
O_5	Prof., exec. or tech.	−4.262 −2	4.409 −2	−9.666 −1	−3.038 −2	−3.112 −2
O_6	Service or other	1.305 −2	3.987 −2	3.274 −1	1.040 −2	1.849 −2
O_7	Skilled laborer	0	0	0	0	0
DN_1	1 dependent(s)	−1.332 −2	4.849 −2	−2.747 −1	−1.119 −2	−2.145 −2
DN_2	2 "	−2.522 −3	4.847 −2	−5.203 −2	−2.340 −3	−5.280 −3
DN_3	3 "	−8.127 −4	5.133 −2	−1.583 −2	−8.300 −4	1.134 −2
DN_4	4 "	2.601 −2	5.291 −2	4.916 −1	2.513 −2	3.732 −2
DN_5	5−6 "	−9.369 −2	5.940 −2	−1.577 +0	−6.782 −2	−7.779 −2
DN_6	7 or more dependents	7.344 −2	9.653 −2	7.609 −1	2.431 −2	1.334 −2
DN_7	No dependents	0	0	0	0	0
SM_1	Married	−8.482 −2	7.004 −2	−1.211 +0	−3.973 −2	−5.378 −2
SM_2	Not married	0	0	0	0	0

AB_1 Borrower age 30–34	−5.629 −3	3.355 −2	−1.678 −1	−5.600 −3	−2.594 −2
AB_2 ,, ,, 35–39	−1.612 −2	3.641 −2	−4.427 −1	−1.506 −2	−2.439 −2
AB_3 ,, ,, 40–44	9.148 −2	4.232 −2	* 2.162 +0	7.099 −2	6.182 −2
AB_4 ,, ,, 45–49	−2.248 −2	5.561 −2	−4.043 −1	−1.238 −2	−3.364 −2
AB_5 ,, ,, 50–59	5.742 −2	5.794 −2	9.910 −1	3.186 −2	−6.960 −3
AB_6 ,, ,, 60 or over	1.161 −2	1.157 −1	1.003 −1	3.030 −3	−4.959 −2
AB_7 ,, ,, 20–29	0	0	0	0	0
R_1 Northeast	4.461 −2	2.036 −1	2.191 −1	5.155 −2	−1.907 −1
R_2 Mid-Atlantic	1.771 −1	2.048 −1	8.646 −1	2.049 −1	1.868 −1
R_3 Southeast	4.987 −1	2.769 −1	1.801 +0	7.424 −2	6.287 −2
R_4 E. N. Central	0				
R_5 E. S. Central	0	No loans included in these regions.			
R_6 W. N. Central	0				
R_7 W. S. Central	0				
R_8 Mountain	0				
R_9 Pacific	0				
TLD_1 LIC	0				
TLD_2 MSB	0				
TLD_3 CB	0				
TLD_4 Trusteed funds	0	All loans made and held by MSB's.			
TLD_5 FNMA	0				
TLD_6 SLA	0				
TLD_7 Own	0				
TLD_8 Individual or other	0				
TLN_1 FHA	3.558 −2	3.945 −2	9.017 −1	3.798 −2	1.301 −1
TLN_2 VA	−5.933 −2	4.093 −2	−1.450 +0	−6.726 −2	−1.035 −2
TLN_3 Conventional	0	0	0	0	0

Note: All numbers within the body of the table are to be multiplied by 10 raised to the exponent indicated in the trailing digit of the number. Thus: 6.962 −2 = (6.962) (10) −2 = .06962. In this table r_{yx} is a simple correlation, not a partial as in the other appendix tables.

TABLE B13

Regression–USSLL:
Current vs. Foreclosed
Constant: −.0104615   N: 5011
R^2 : .0505   FOR: 6.53**
S_e : .0138

Variable Symbol	Variable Name	b	S_b	b/S_b	β	r_{yx}
RLS	Loan/Value ratio	2482 –2	1655 –2	1499 +0	2603 –2	2126 –2
T	Init. term to maturity	1054 –4	4174 –3	2525 +0 **	4631 –2	3579 –2
RPI	Payment/Income ratio	3075 –2	3936 –0	7812 –1	1183 –2	1108 –2
O_1	Self employed	4685 –3	5957 –1	7865 –1	1305 –2	1116 –2
O_2	Executive or manager	4427 –3	6483 –1	6829 –1	1118 –2	9686 –3
O_3	Sales	1454 –2	8390 –1	1733 +0	2609 –2	2457 –2
O_4	White collar	−5341 –3	6399 –1	−8346 –1	−1340 –2	−1184 –2
O_5	Unskilled labor	−7040 –3	7585 –1	−9282 –1	−1418 –2	−1317 –2
O_6	Professional	−9598 –3	1651 –2	−5813 –1	−8379 –3	−8245 –3
O_7	Government service	2 689 –2	1699 –2	1582 +0	2356 –2	2243 –2
O_8	Other	−3309 –3	9409 –1	−3517 –1	− 5355 –3	−4988 –3
O_9	Skilled labor	0	0	0	0	0
DN_1	1 dependent(s)	1448 –2	1292 –2	1120 +0	4925 –2	1588 –2
DN_2	2 ,,	1268 –2	1350 0	9391 –1	3 605 –2	1332 –2
DN_3	3 ,,	2127 –2	13 66 –2	1557 +0	6004 –2	2208 –2
DN_4	4 ,,	2477 –2	1446 –2	1712 +0	5127 –2	2427 –2
DN_5	5–6 ,,	1740 –2	1539 –2	1130 +0	2872 –2	1602 –2
DN_6	7–8 ,,	3009 –2	2321 –2	1296 +0	2165 –2	1837 –2
DN_7	9 or more dependents	1898 –3	3176 0	5976 –2	9061 –4	8476 –4
DN_8	No dependents	0	0	0	0	0

130

		Col 1	Col 2	Col 3	Col 4	Col 5
SM_1	Married	-2116 -2	1383 -2	-1530 +0	-4053 -2	-2169 -2
SM_2	Widowed	-6718 -3	1712 -2	-3924 -1	-7064 -3	-5566 -3
SM_3	Divorced	-1902 -4	1864 -3	-1020 -1	-1722 -4	-1447 -4
SM_4	Single	0	0	0	0	0
AB_1	Borrower age 30–34	-1414 -2	7152 -1	*-1977 +0	-3735 -2	-2803 -2
AB_2	" 35–39	-9905 -3	7085 -3	-1398 +0	-2714 -2	-1983 -2
AB_3	" 40–44	-4569 -3	7310 -1	-6250 -1	-1190 -2	-8866 -3
AB_4	" 45–49	-3355 -3	7524 -1	-4459 -1	-8438 -3	-6324 -3
AB_5	" 50–54	-3779 -3	8413 -1	-4492 -1	-7982 -3	-6871 -3
AB_6	" 55–59	-1789 -2	1044 -2	-1713 +0	-2805 -2	-2430 -2
AB_7	" 60 and over	-1037 -2	1135 -1	-9136 -1	-1547 -2	-1296 -2
AB_8	" 20–29	0	0	0	0	0
P_1	Construction	2823 -2	5491 -1	** 5141 +0	7882 -2	7274 -2
P_2	Repair	2443 -2	9919 -1	** 2463 +0	3681 -2	3492 -2
P_3	Refinance	2074 -2	5405 -1	** 3837 +0	6181 -2	5434 -2
P_4	Purchase	0	0	0	0	0
FJ_1	Jr. financing	5204 -2	5527 -1	** 9416 +0	1451 -1	1324 -1
FJ_2	No jr. financing	0	0	0	0	0
R_1	Northeast	-6709 -3	9823 -1	-6830 -1	-1156 -2	-9688 -3
R_2	Mid-Atlantic	-3833 -2	7989 -1	*-4798 +0	-9864 -2	-6790 -2
R_3	Southeast	-1377 -2	8086 -1	-1703 +0	-3048 -2	-2415 -2
R_4	E. N. Central	-2430 -2	6778 -1	**-3585 +0	-8185 -2	-5079 -2
R_5	E. S. Central	-3922 -2	1652 -2	**-2372 +0	-35 67 -3	-3364 -2
R_6	W. N. Central	-4098 -2	7755 -1	**-5284 +0	-1015 -1	-7475 -2
R_7	W. S. Central	-2620 -2	1170 -2	**-2239 +0	-3586 -2	-3175 -2
R_8	Mountain	-4598 -2	1689 -2	**-2721 +0	-3974 -2	-3557 -2
R_9	Pacific	0	0	0	0	0

Note: All numbers within the body of the table are to be multiplied by 10 raised to the exponent indicated in the trailing digit of the number. Thus: $6.962 \cdot -2 = .06962. \quad 10)^{-2} = .06962.$

131

Explanation of Lorenz Tables

Tables B14 through B26 contain the values which were used to plot the Lorenz curves in the body of the monograph. Headings at the top of each column are largely self explanatory. The column on the far left of each table shows the actual range of values obtained from each of the regression equations when the observations were fed in. It should be noted that these values were broken up into intervals of .02 for plotting purposes. The column labeled (1) shows the weighted total number of observations having the indicated index value. Column (2) is merely the cumulation of column (1), and column (3) indicates the proportion of observations having an index value less than or equal to the one indicated in the left-hand column. Columns (4), (5), and (6) are calculated on the same basis as columns (1), (2), and (3), but the observations in those columns pertain to the subset, e.g., noncurrent loans, representative of the risk being measured.

TABLE B14

USSLL:
Lorenz–Current vs. Noncurrent

Index Value	(1) Weighted Total Observations	(2) Cumulative Total Observations	(3) Ratio: (2)/Total (2)	(4) Weighted Noncurrent Observations	(5) Cumulative Noncurrent Observations	(6) Ratio: (5)/Total (5)
−.26	3.3	3.3	.000	0	0	0
−.24	1.6	4.9	.000	0	0	0
−.22	7.7	12.6	.001	0	0	0
−.20	12.5	25.1	.001	0	0	0
−.18	13.7	38.8	.002	0	0	0
−.16	37.7	76.5	.004	0	0	0
−.14	35.0	111.5	.006	0	0	0
−.12	121.8	233.3	.012	17.5	17.5	.004
−.10	94.4	327.7	.017	0	17.5	.004
−.08	241.9	569.6	.029	4.4	21.9	.005
−.06	323.5	893.1	.045	0	21.9	.005
−.04	313.8	1206.9	.061	0	21.9	.005
−.02	375.8	1582.7	.080	0	21.9	.005
−.00	445.9	2028.6	.103	0	21.9	.005
.02	421.2	2449.8	.124	0	21.9	.005
.04	503.2	2953.0	.150	34.2	56.1	.013

(continued)

133

TABLE B 14 (continued)

Index Value	(1) Weighted Total Observations	(2) Cumulative Total Observations	(3) Ratio: (2)/Total (2)	(4) Weighted Noncurrent Observations	(5) Cumulative Noncurrent Observations	(6) Ratio: (5)/Total (5)
.06	639.4	3592.4	.182	19.9	76.0	.017
.08	703.4	4295.8	.218	78.4	154.4	.035
.10	710.3	5006.1	.254	75.6	230.0	.052
.12	766.8	5772.9	.293	45.1	272.1	.062
.14	827.1	6500.0	.330	90.6	365.7	.082
.16	866.9	7466.9	.379	113.8	479.5	.108
.18	937.9	8404.8	.429	169.9	649.4	.146
.20	965.1	9369.9	.475	203.0	852.4	.191
.22	867.2	10237.1	.519	210.6	1063.0	.238
.24	1099.6	11336.7	.575	337.6	1400.6	.314
.26	1016.1	12352.8	.627	230.4	1631.0	.366
.28	978.4	13331.2	.676	217.9	1848.9	.415
.30	912.9	14244.1	.723	252.4	2101.3	.471
.32	872.1	15116.2	.767	339.6	2440.9	.547
.34	823.2	15939.4	.809	308.9	2749.8	.617
.36	905.5	16844.9	.855	339.7	3089.5	.693
.38	777.0	17621.9	.894	366.7	3456.2	.775
.40	651.9	18273.3	.927	341.0	3797.2	.852
.42	423.4	18697.2	.949	203.8	4001.0	.897
.44	323.8	19021.0	.965	153.0	4154.0	.932

.46	210.6	19231.6	.976	118.2	4272.2	.958
.48	178.7	19410.3	.985	38.0	4310.2	.967
.50	95.7	19506.0	.990	36.2	4346.4	.975
.52	68.6	19574.6	.993	34.3	4380.7	.982
.54	59.8	19634.4	.996	21.7	4402.4	.987
.56	29.0	196 63.4	.998	27.0	4429.4	.993
.58	29.9	19693.3	.999	15.9	4445.3	.997
.60	14.4	19708.7	1.000	12.3	4457.6	1.000
.62	0	19708.7	1.000	0	4457.6	1.000
.64	0	19708.7	1.000	0	4457.6	1.000
.66	0	19708.7	1.000	0	4457.6	1.000
.68	0	19708.7	1.000	0	4457.6	1.000
.70	1.7	19708.4	1.000	1.7	4459.3	1.000

TABLE B15

MBA:
Lorenz–Current vs. Noncurrent

Index Value	Weighted Total Observations	Cumulative Total Observations	Ratio: (2)/Total (2)	Weighted Noncurrent Observations	Cumulative Noncurrent Observations	Ratio: (5)/Total (5)
−.04	1.0	1.0	.000	0	0	.000
−.02	0	1.0	.000	0	0	.000
.00	0	1.0	.000	0	0	.000
.02	4.0	5.0	.001	4.0	4.0	.001
.04	3.0	8.0	.001	0	4.0	.001
.06	2.0	10.0	.001	0	4.0	.001
.08	0	10.0	.001	0	4.0	.001
.10	3.0	13.0	.001	2.0	6.0	.001
.12	5.0	18.0	.002	0	6.0	.001
.14	9.0	27.0	.003	0	6.0	.001
.16	3.0	30.0	.003	0	6.0	.001
.18	8.0	38.0	.004	0	6.0	.001
.20	4.0	42.0	.004	2.0	8.0	.002
.22	14.0	56.0	.006	6.0	14.0	.003
.24	38.0	94.0	.010	5.0	19.0	.004
.26	43.0	137.0	.014	11.0	30.0	.006
.28	57.0	194.0	.020	8.0	38.0	.008
.30	89.0	283.0	.030	37.0	75.0	.016
.32	156.0	439.0	.046	57.0	132.0	.228
.34	176.0	615.0	.065	38.0	170.0	.036

136

.36	206.0	821.0	.087	61.0	231.0	.049
.38	297.0	1118.0	.118	153.0	384.0	.081
.40	406.0	1524.0	.161	140.0	524.0	.111
.42	577.0	2101.0	.222	244.0	768.0	.162
.44	502.0	2603.0	.274	191.0	959.0	.203
.46	643.0	3246.0	.342	276.0	1235.0	.261
.48	827.0	4073.0	.430	422.0	1657.0	.350
.50	886.0	4959.0	.523	466.0	2123.0	.449
.52	952.0	5911.0	.623	555.0	2678.0	.566
.54	763.0	6674.0	.704	353.0	3031.0	.641
.56	657.0	7331.0	.773	340.0	3371.0	.713
.58	675.0	8006.0	.844	440.0	3811.0	.806
.60	428.0	8434.0	.890	249.0	4060.0	.859
.62	369.0	8803.0	.928	237.0	4297.0	.909
.64	241.0	9044.0	.954	150.0	4447.0	.941
.66	177.0	9221.0	.975	103.0	4550.0	.962
.68	95.0	9316.0	.983	73.0	4623.0	.978
.70	93.0	9409.0	.992	60.0	4683.0	.990
.72	30.0	9439.0	.996	14.0	4697.0	.993
.74	19.0	9458.0	.998	12.0	4709.0	.996
.76	0	9458.0	.998	0	4709.0	.996
.78	8.0	9466.0	.998	5.0	4714.0	.997
.80	12.0	9478.0	1.000	11.0	4725.0	.999
.82	0	9478.0	1.000	0	4725.0	.999
.84	0	9478.0	1.000	0	4725.0	.900
.86	2.0	9480.0	1.000	2.0	4727.0	1.000
.88	1.0	9481.0	1.000	1.0	4728.0	1.000

NAMSB:
Lorenz–Current vs. Noncurrent

Index Value	Weighted Total Observations	Cumulative Total Observations	Ratio: (2)/Total (2)	Weighted Noncurrent Observations	Cumulative Noncurrent Observations	Ratio: (5)/Total (5)
+ .16	0	0	.000	0	0	.000
.18	4	4	.001	2	2	.001
.20	1	5	.001	0	2	.001
.22	7	12	.002	0	2	.001
.24	12	24	.004	0	2	.001
.26	29	53	.010	9	11	.004
.28	32	85	.016	24	35	.013
.30	49	134	.025	15	50	.019
.32	80	215	.040	30	80	.030
.34	135	349	.066	39	119	.044
.36	129	478	.090	50	169	.063
.38	210	688	.129	89	258	.097
.40	207	895	.169	83	341	.128
.42	339	1234	.232	128	469	.176
.44	417	1651	.310	156	625	.234
.46	407	2058	.387	182	807	.302
.48	441	2499	.469	180	987	.370
.50	348	2847	.535	204	1191	.446

.52	373	3220	.605	187	1378	.516
.54	294	3514	.660	145	1523	.570
.56	270	3784	.711	118	1641	.615
.58	315	4099	.770	210	1851	.693
.60	247	4346	.816	143	1994	.747
.62	250	4596	.863	173	2167	.812
.64	167	4763	.895	111	2278	.853
.66	119	4882	.917	71	2349	.880
.68	119	5001	.940	93	2442	.915
.70	111	5112	.960	75	2517	.943
.72	79	5191	.975	66	2583	.967
.74	45	5236	.984	28	2611	.978
.76	50	5286	.993	31	2642	.990
.78	24	5310	.998	17	2659	.996
.80	7	5317	.999	6	2665	.998
.82	6	5323	1.000	5	2670	1.000

TABLE B17

USSLL:
Lorenz–Current vs. Noncurrent (Pooled)

Index Value	Weighted Total Observations	Cumulative Total Observations	Ratio: (2)/Total (2)	Weighted Noncurrent Observations	Cumulative Noncurrent Observations	Ratio: (5)/Total (5)
−.22	3.3	3.3	.000	0	0	0
−.20	15.3	18.6	.001	0	0	0
−.18	1.6	20.2	.001	0	0	0
−.16	6.1	26.3	.001	0	0	0
−.14	20.2	46.5	.002	0	0	0
−.12	33.9	80.4	.003	0	0	0
−.10	83.0	163.4	.007	0	0	0
−.08	146.2	309.6	.013	20.7	20.7	.004
−.06	265.0	574.6	.024	23.6	44.3	.008
−.04	349.8	924.4	.039	0	44.3	.008
−.02	275.5	1199.9	.051	0	44.3	.008
−.00	465.1	1665.0	.071	0	44.3	.008
.02	496.4	2161.4	.092	9.8	54.1	.010
.04	501.7	2663.1	.113	0	54.1	.010
.06	63 6.6	3299.7	.140	5.8	59.9	.011
.08	582.2	3881.9	.165	27.6	87.5	.016
.10	865.7	4747.6	.202	111.8	199.3	.037
.12	744.6	5492.2	.234	122.0	321.3	.060

.14	910.9	6403.1	.272	131.9	453.2	.084
.16	968.7	7371.8	.314	145.4	598.6	.111
.18	1059.1	8430.9	.359	211.7	803.1	.149
.20	1302.2	9733.1	.414	193.1	1003.4	.186
.22	1372.3	11105.4	.473	264.1	1267.5	.235
.24	1499.6	12605.0	.536	377.2	1644.7	.305
.26	1744.8	14349.8	.611	472.7	2117.4	.393
.28	1738.3	16088.1	.685	430.3	2547.7	.473
.30	1764.3	17852.4	.760	615.9	3163.6	.587
.32	1604.8	19457.2	.828	637.3	3800.9	.706
.34	1236.5	20693.7	.881	443.0	4243.9	.788
.36	940.0	21633.7	.921	386.8	4630.7	.860
.38	779.7	22413.4	.954	296.7	4927.4	.915
.40	459.1	22872.5	.973	170.5	5097.9	.946
.42	289.3	23161.8	.986	122.6	5220.5	.969
.44	178.1	23339.9	.993	66.1	5286.6	.982
.46	81.6	23421.5	.997	31.5	5318.1	.987
.48	46.7	23468.2	.999	44.0	5362.1	.996
.50	19.8	23488.0	1.000	19.8	5381.9	.999
.52	4.6	23492.6	1.000	1.7	5383.6	1.000
.54	3.1	23495.7	1.000	2.0	5385.6	1.000
.56	1.1	23496.8	1.000	0	5385.6	1.000

TABLE B18

MBA:
Lorenz—Current vs. Noncurrent (Pooled)

Index Value	Weighted Total Observations	Cumulative Total Observations	Ratio: (2)/Total(2)	Weighted Noncurrent Observations	Cumulative Noncurrent Observations	Ratio: (5)/Total(5)
.04	2	2	0	1	1	.000
.06	2	4	0	0	1	.000
.08	1	5	.001	0	1	.000
.10	8	13	.001	4	5	.001
.12	7	20	.002	0	5	.001
.14	2	22	.002	1	6	.001
.16	5	27	.003	0	6	.001
.18	12	39	.004	7	13	.003
.20	18	57	.006	5	18	.004
.22	18	75	.008	6	24	.005
.24	26	101	.011	4	28	.006
.26	25	126	.013	14	42	.009
.28	72	198	.021	24	66	.014
.30	63	261	.028	12	78	.016
.32	91	352	.037	43	121	.026
.34	170	522	.055	46	167	.035
.36	229	751	.079	91	258	.055
.38	240	991	.104	93	351	.074

.40	461	1452	.153	141	492	.104
.42	497	1949	.206	245	737	.157
.44	627	2576	.272	202	939	.199
.46	710	3286	.347	349	1288	.272
.48	778	4064	.430	381	1669	.353
.50	879	4943	.521	489	2158	.456
.52	780	5723	.604	420	2578	.545
.54	840	6563	.692	419	2997	.634
.56	748	7311	.771	400	3397	.718
.58	580	7891	.832	345	3742	.791
.60	545	8346	.890	316	4058	.858
.62	414	8850	.933	240	4298	.909
.64	170	9020	.951	108	4406	.932
.66	211	9231	.974	169	4575	.968
.68	95	9326	.984	52	4627	.979
.70	98	9424	.994	67	4694	.993
.72	34	9458	.998	27	4721	.998
.74	18	9476	.999	3	4724	.999
.76	3	9479	1.000	2	4726	1.000
.78	2	9481	1.000	2	4728	1.000

TABLE B19

NAMSB:
Lorenz–Current vs. Noncurrent (Pooled)

Index Value	Weighted Total Observations	Cumulative Total Observations	Ratio: (2)/Total(2)	Weighted Noncurrent Observations	Cumulative Noncurrent Observations	Ratio: (5)/Total(5)
+.16	2	2	.000	0	0	.000
.18	2	4	.001	2	2	.001
.20	3	7	.001	0	2	.001
.22	4	11	.002	0	2	.001
.24	11	22	.004	0	2	.001
.26	19	41	.008	3	5	.002
.28	17	58	.011	8	13	.005
.30	76	134	.025	39	52	.019
.32	57	191	.036	26	78	.029
.34	94	285	.054	16	94	.035
.36	192	477	.090	84	178	.067
.38	161	638	.120	84	262	.098
.40	239	877	.165	70	332	.124
.42	297	1174	.220	121	453	.170
.44	440	1614	.303	143	596	.223
.46	418	2032	.382	191	787	.295
.48	491	2523	.474	212	999	.374
.50	377	2900	.545	217	1216	.455

.52	329	3229	.607	169	1385	.519
.54	274	3503	.658	143	1528	.572
.56	318	3821	.718	154	1682	.630
.58	266	4087	.768	151	1833	.686
.60	276	4363	.820	188	2021	.757
.62	262	4625	.869	172	2193	.821
.64	181	4806	.903	125	2318	.868
.66	128	4934	.227	75	2393	.896
.68	75	5009	.941	51	2444	.915
.70	107	5116	.961	75	2519	.943
.72	86	5202	.977	66	2585	.968
.74	70	5272	.990	39	2624	.983
.76	27	5299	.995	23	2647	.991
.78	12	5311	.998	11	2658	.996
.80	9	5320	.999	9	2667	.999
.82	3	5323	1.000	3	2670	1.000

TABLE B20

USSLL:
Lorenz–Delinquent vs. Foreclosures

Index Value	Weighted Total Delinquent Observations	Cumulative Total Observations	Ratio: (2)/Total(2)	Weighted Number Foreclosures	Cumulative Foreclosures	Ratio: (5)/Total(5)
-.14	9.4	9.4	.002	0	0	.000
-.12	1.1	10.5	.002	0	0	.000
-.10	29.4	39.9	.009	0	0	.000
-.08	18.2	58.1	.013	0	0	.000
-.06	97.6	155.7	.035	0	0	.000
-.04	170.0	325.7	.073	0	0	.000
-.02	237.6	563.3	.126	1.9	1.9	.007
.00	466.5	1029.8	.231	0	1.9	.007
.02	468.4	1498.2	.336	0	1.9	.007
.04	556.0	2054.2	.461	4.1	6.0	.022
.06	341.4	2395.6	.537	0	6.0	.022
.08	415.1	2810.7	.630	22.1	28.1	.106
.10	288.9	3099.6	.695	14.2	42.3	.159
.12	258.8	3358.4	.753	6.4	48.7	.183
.14	231.5	3589.9	.805	7.3	56.0	.211
.16	213.0	3802.9	.853	19.0	75.0	.282
.18	152.8	3955.7	.887	28.4	103.4	.389
.20	168.3	4124.0	.925	38.2	141.6	.533

.22	72.3	4196.3	.941	17.0	158.6	.597
.24	63.0	4259.3	.955	18.6	177.2	.667
.26	41.0	4300.3	.964	12.0	189.2	.712
.28	19.8	4320.1	.969	12.0	201.2	.757
.30	16.6	4336.7	.972	2.6	203.8	.767
.32	5.7	4342.4	.974	5.7	209.5	.788
.34	26.8	4369.2	.980	15.5	225.0	.847
.36	40.8	4410.0	.989	21.1	246.1	.926
.38	19.7	4429.7	.993	9.8	255.9	.963
.40	19.7	4449.4	.998	9.8	265.7	1.000
.42	0	4449.4	.998	0	265.7	1.000
.44	0	4449.4	.998	0	265.7	1.000
.46	9.8	4459.2	1.000	0	265.7	1.000

TABLE B21

MBA:

Lorenz—Delinquent vs. Foreclosures

Index Value	Weighted Total Delinquent Observations	Cumulative Total Observations	Ratio: (2)/Total(2)	Weighted Number Foreclosures	Cumulative Foreclosures	Ratio: (5)/Total(5)
.02	1	1	.000	0	0	.000
.04	3	4	.001	0	0	.000
.06	12	16	.003	0	0	.000
.08	1	17	.004	1	1	.000
.10	8	25	.005	0	1	.000
.12	1	26	.005	0	1	.000
.14	14	40	.008	0	1	.000
.16	6	46	.010	2	3	.001
.18	2	48	.010	3	6	.002
.20	14	62	.013	4	10	.004
.22	20	82	.017	3	13	.005
.24	21	103	.022	10	23	.009
.26	48	151	.032	17	41	.016
.28	63	214	.045	7	48	.019
.30	36	250	.053	7	55	.022
.32	41	291	.062	36	91	.037
.34	99	390	.082	28	119	.048
.36	104	494	.104	126	245	.099
.38	210	704	.149	35	280	.113
.40	132	836	.177	62	342	.138
.42	232	1068	.226	70	412	.170
.44	182	1250	.264			

.46	294	1544	.326	148	569	.229
.48	317	1861	.394	178	747	.301
.50	324	2185	.462	174	921	.371
.52	313	2498	.528	182	1103	.445
.54	395	2893	.612	218	1321	.533
.56	412	3305	.699	216	1537	.620
.58	247	3552	.751	144	1681	.678
.60	213	3765	.796	105	1786	.720
.62	221	3986	.843	157	1943	.783
.64	185	4171	.882	125	2068	.834
.66	135	4306	.911	82	2150	.867
.68	112	4418	.934	86	2236	.902
.70	113	4531	.958	85	2321	.936
.72	51	4582	.969	39	2360	.952
.74	50	4632	.980	34	2394	.965
.76	20	4652	.984	16	2410	.972
.78	7	4659	.985	3	2413	.973
.80	4	4663	.986	4	2417	.974
.82	7	4670	.988	7	2424	.977
.84	16	4686	.991	16	2440	.984
.86	1	4687	.991	1	2441	.984
.88	4	4691	.992	2	2443	.985
.90	12	4703	.995	12	2455	.990
.92	2	4705	.995	2	2457	.991
.94	2	4707	.996	2	2459	.992
.96	0	4707	.996	0	2459	.992
.98	10	4717	.998	10	2469	.996
1.00	0	4717	.998	0	2469	.996
1.02	11	4728	1.000	11	2480	1.000

TABLE B22

NAMSB:

Lorenz–Delinquent vs. Foreclosures

Index Value	Weighted Total Delinquent Observations	Cumulative Total Observations	Ratio: (2)/Total(2)	Weighted Number Foreclosures	Cumulative Foreclosures	Ratio: (5)/Total(5)
−.18	6	6	.002	0	0	.000
−.16	0	6	.002	0	0	.000
−.14	2	8	.003	0	0	.000
−.12	2	10	.004	0	0	.000
−.10	0	10	.004	0	0	.000
−.08	17	27	.010	0	0	.000
−.06	5	32	.012	0	0	.000
−.04	9	41	.015	2	2	.003
−.02	11	52	.019	0	2	.003
.00	13	65	.024	0	2	.003
.02	22	87	.033	0	2	.003
.04	32	119	.044	0	2	.003
.06	34	153	.057	4	6	.010
.08	62	215	.081	5	11	.018
.10	89	304	.114	6	17	.028
.12	146	450	.168	16	33	.055
.14	136	586	.219	11	44	.073
.16	114	700	.262	30	74	.123
.18	129	829	.310	16	90	.150
.20	140	969	.363	31	121	.201
.22	145	1114	.417	23	144	.239
.24	141	1255	.470	47	191	.317

.26	133	1388	.520	36	227	.377
.28	154	1542	.578	19	246	.409
.30	155	1697	.636	39	285	.473
.32	148	1845	.691	10	295	.490
.34	186	2031	.761	53	348	.579
.36	137	2168	.812	46	394	.654
.38	154	2322	.870	63	457	.759
.40	96	2418	.906	28	584	.806
.42	63	2481	.929	24	509	.846
.44	42	2523	.445	24	533	.885
.46	68	2591	.970	36	569	.945
.48	21	2612	.978	6	575	.955
.50	2	2614	.979	0	575	.955
.52	9	2623	.982	5	580	.963
.54	4	2627	.984	4	584	.970
.56	4	2631	.985	1	585	.972
.58	0	2631	.985	0	585	.972
.60	1	2632	.986	1	586	.973
.62	7	2639	.988	0	586	.973
.64	2	2641	.989	1	587	.975
.66	5	2646	.991	2	589	.978
.68	3	2649	.992	3	592	.983
.70	1	2650	.993	1	593	.985
.72	1	2651	.993	0	593	.985
.74	0	2651	.993	0	593	.985
.76	0	2651	.993	0	593	.985
.78	0	2651	.993	0	593	.985
.80	0	2651	.993	0	593	.985
.82	0	2651	.993	0	593	.985
.84	0	2651	.993	0	593	.985
.86	0	2651	.993	0	593	.985

(continued)

151

TABLE B 22 (concluded)

Index Value	Weighted Total Delinquent Observations	Cumulative Total Observations	Ratio: (2)/Total(2)	Weighted Number Foreclosures	Cumulative Foreclosures	Ratio: (5)/Total(5)
.88	1	2652	.993	1	594	.987
.90	0	2652	.993	0	594	.987
.92	0	2652	.993	0	594	.987
.94	3	2652	.993	0	594	.987
.96	0	2655	.994	3	597	.992
.98	0	2655	.994	0	597	.992
1.00	0	2655	.994	0	597	.992
1.02	5	2655	.994	0	597	.992
1.04	0	2660	.996	0	597	.992
1.06	5	2660	.996	0	597	.992
1.08	3	2665	.998	5	602	1.000
1.10	0	2668	.999	0	602	1.000
1.12	0	2668	.999	0	602	1.000
1.14	2	2668	.999	0	602	1.000
1.16		2670	1.000	0	602	1.000

TABLE B23

USSLL:
Lorenz—Delinquent vs. Foreclosures (Pooled)

lex lue	Weighted Total Delinquent Observations	Cumulative Total Observations	Ratio: (2)/Total(2)	Weighted Number Foreclosures	Cumulative Foreclosures	Ratio: (5)/Total(5)
14	1.0	1.1	.000	0	0	.000
12	0.0	1.1	.000	0	0	.000
10	1.1	2.2	.000	0	0	.000
08	8.3	10.5	.002	0	0	.000
06	95.8	106.3	.020	0	0	.000
04	144.6	250.9	.046	0	0	.000
02	213.8	464.7	.086	0	0	.000
00	455.2	919.9	.171	0	0	.000
02	670.2	1590.1	.295	14.3	14.3	.037
04	773.9	2364.0	.439	10.9	25.2	.066
06	557.4	2921.4	.542	1.9	27.1	.071
08	468.1	3389.5	.629	35.4	62.5	.163
10	400.3	3789.8	.704	35.5	98.0	.256
12	288.6	4078.4	.757	23.4	121.4	.317
14	246.5	4324.9	.803	16.7	138.1	.360
16	290.1	4615.0	.857	41.3	179.4	.468
18	211.2	4826.2	.896	34.2	213.6	.557
20	234.2	5060.4	.940	65.5	279.1	.728
22	75.7	5136.1	.954	22.5	301.6	.787
24	78.5	5214.6	.968	15.3	316.9	.826
26	26.5	5241.1	.973	6.4	323.3	.843
28	13.5	5254.6	.976	5.7	329.0	.858
30	19.0	5273.6	.979	11.3	340.3	.888
32	3.8	5277.4	.980	3.8	344.1	.897
34	9.8	5287.2	.982	0.0	344.1	.897
36	39.3	5226.5	.989	29.5	373.6	.974
38	29.5	5356.0	.994	9.8	383.4	1.000
40	9.8	5365.8	.996	0.0	383.4	1.000
42	19.7	5385.5	1.000	0.0	383.4	1.000

TABLE B24

MBA:
Lorenz–Delinquent vs. Foreclosures (Pooled)

Index Value	Weighted Total Delinquent Observations	Cumulative Total Observations	Ratio: (2)/Total(2)	Weighted Number Foreclosures	Cumulative Foreclosures	Ratio: (5)/Total(5)
−.08	3	3	.000	0	0	.000
−.06	0	3	.000	0	0	.000
−.04	4	7	.001	3	3	.001
−.02	3	10	.001	0	3	.001
.00	0	10	.001	0	3	.001
.02	7	17	.002	0	3	.001
.04	0	17	.002	4	3	.001
.06	4	21	.002	0	7	.001
.08	2	23	.002	5	7	.001
.10	5	28	.003	0	12	.002
.12	1	29	.003	4	12	.002
.14	12	41	.004	4	16	.003
.16	14	55	.006	4	20	.004
.18	13	68	.007	4	24	.005
.20	49	117	.012	41	65	.014
.22	31	148	.016	11	76	.016
.24	15	163	.017	0	76	.016
.26	83	246	.026	25	101	.021
.28	76	322	.034	43	144	.030
.30	91	413	.044	55	199	.042
.32	125	538	.057	50	249	.053

154

.34	172	710	.075	104	353	.075
.36	197	907	.096	118	471	.096
.38	253	1160	.122	121	592	.125
.40	359	1519	.160	190	782	.165
.42	445	1964	.207	205	987	.209
.44	536	2500	.264	297	1284	.271
.46	537	3037	.320	288	1572	.332
.48	589	3626	.382	241	1813	.384
.50	617	4243	.448	302	2115	.447
.52	709	4952	.522	372	2487	.526
.54	641	5593	.590	322	2809	.594
.56	648	6241	.658	321	3130	.662
.58	521	6662	.703	269	3399	.719
.60	587	7349	.775	265	3664	.775
.62	614	7963	.840	320	3984	.843
.64	440	8403	.886	198	4182	.885
.66	347	8750	.923	184	4366	.924
.68	259	9009	.950	104	4474	.946
.70	171	9180	.968	93	4567	.966
.72	106	9286	.979	52	4619	.977
.74	110	9396	.991	71	4690	.992
.76	47	9443	.996	22	4712	.997
.78	4	9447	.996	3	4715	.997
.80	16	9463	.998	4	4719	.998
.82	9	9472	.999	8	4727	1.000
.84	1	9473	.999	0	4727	1.000
.86	8	9481	1.000	0	4727	1.000

TABLE B25

NAMSB:
Lorenz–Delinquent vs. Foreclosures (Pooled)

Index Value	Weighted Total Delinquent Observations	Cumulative Total Observations	Ratio: (2)/Total(2)	Weighted Number Foreclosures	Cumulative Foreclosures	Ratio: (5)/Total(5)
−.14	4	4	.001	0	0	.000
−.12	0	4	.001	0	0	.000
−.10	0	4	.001	0	0	.000
−.08	0	4	.001	0	0	.000
−.06	3	7	.003	0	0	.000
−.04	3	10	.004	0	0	.000
−.02	9	19	.007	0	0	.000
.00	11	30	.011	0	0	.000
.02	34	64	.024	4	4	.007
.04	32	96	.036	3	7	.012
.06	46	142	.053	1	8	.013
.08	74	216	.081	12	20	.033
.10	90	306	.115	6	26	.043
.12	83	389	.146	6	32	.053
.14	87	476	.178	12	44	.073
.16	105	581	.218	13	57	.095
.18	160	741	.278	13	90	.153
.20	144	885	.331	35	105	.174
.22	122	1007	.377	24	129	.214

.24	148	1155	.432	42	171	.284
.26	131	1286	.482	36	207	.344
.28	201	1487	.557	57	264	.439
.30	209	1696	.635	26	290	.482
.32	157	1853	.694	41	331	.550
.34	208	2061	.772	52	383	.636
.36	152	2213	.829	59	442	.734
.38	191	2404	.900	55	497	.826
.40	95	2499	.936	30	527	.875
.42	38	2537	.950	14	541	.899
.44	34	2571	.963	7	548	.910
.46	55	2626	.984	40	588	.977
.48	9	2635	.987	0	588	.977
.50	6	2641	.989	4	592	.983
.52	4	2645	.991	0	592	.983
.54	7	2652	.993	0	592	.983
.56	3	2655	.994	0	592	.983
.58	1	2656	.995	1	593	.985
.60	0	2656	.995	0	593	.985
.62	1	2657	.995	1	594	.987
.64	1	2658	.996	0	594	.987
.66	5	2663	.997	2	596	.990
.68	1	2664	.998	0	596	.990
.70	2	2666	.999	2	598	.993
.72	2	2668	.999	2	600	.997
.74	1	2669	1.000	1	601	.998
.76	1	2670	1.000	1	602	1.000

TABLE B26

USSLL:
Lorenz—Current vs. Foreclosed

Index Value	Weighted Total Observations	Cumulative Total Observations	Ratio: (2)/Total(2)	Weighted Foreclosure Observations	Cumulative Foreclosure Observations	Ratio: (5)/Total(5)
−.06	1.1	1.1	.000	0.0	0.0	.0
−.04	103.3	104.4	.007	0.0	0.0	.0
−.02	1007.1	1111.5	.072	0.0	0.0	.0
.00	3458.3	4569.8	.295	1.9	1.9	.007
.02	4411.8	8981.6	.579	1.9	3.8	.014
.04	3385.2	12366.8	.797	62.4	66.2	.249
.06	1647.1	14013.9	.903	29.6	95.8	.360
.08	840.9	14854.8	.957	61.2	157.0	.590
.10	393.0	15247.8	.983	46.8	203.8	.767
.12	219.6	15467.4	.997	48.1	251.9	.948
.14	37.1	15504.5	.999	13.9	265.8	1.000
.16	11.3	15515.8	1.000	0.0	265.8	1.000

Appendix C

Regression Equations for Calculating Risk Indexes

The equations which were used to calculate risk indexes through time are listed below. The first term on the right-hand side of each equation is the constant. This is followed by the regression coefficient and mnemonic symbol of each variable included in the equations. Standard errors of the regression coefficients appear in parentheses directly below the coefficients to which they apply.

Delinquency Risk

CONVENTIONAL LOANS

Sample Data

$$R = .3026 + .1694RLS - .00034T + .04148P_1$$
$$(.0420) \quad\ (.0001) \quad\ (.0139)$$
$$+ .1191P_2 + .1641P_3 + .1830FJ$$
$$(.0247) \quad\ (.0133) \quad\ (.0136)$$

Aggregate Data

$$R = .3509 + .1824RLS - .00046T + .0513P_1 + .1570P_2$$
$$(.0487) \quad\ (.0001) \quad\ (.0141) \quad\ (.0140)$$

FHA AND VA LOANS (SAMPLE AND AGGREGATE DATA)

$$R = .2972 + .4451RLS - .00055T - .1002RPI$$
$$(.0812) \quad\ (.00016) \quad\ (.1808)$$

Conditional Foreclosure Risk

CONVENTIONAL LOANS

Sample Data

$$R = .0943 + .0704RLS + .00049T + .0852P_1$$
$$(.0532) \quad (.00013) \quad (.0190)$$
$$+ .0484P_2 + .0560P_3 + .0741FJ$$
$$(.0302) \quad (.0167) \quad (.0221)$$

Aggregate Data

$$R = .1198 + .0432RLS + .00054T + .0872P_1 + .0541P_2$$
$$(.0201) \quad (.0001) \quad (.0187) \quad (.0231)$$

FHA AND VA LOANS (SAMPLE AND AGGREGATE DATA)

$$R = - .0618 + .2916RLS + .00051T - .5121RPI$$
$$(.1022) \quad (.00019) \quad (.2167)$$

Straight Foreclosure Risk (Conventional Loans)

SAMPLE DATA

$$R = .1574 + .0400RLS + .0012T + .0285P_1$$
$$(.0160) \quad (.0004) \quad (.0053)$$
$$+ .0244P_2 + .0274P_3 + .0579FJ$$
$$(.0098) \quad (.0053) \quad (.0052)$$

AGGREGATE DATA

$$R = .1331 + .0473RLS + .0023T + .0293P_1 + .0513P_2$$
$$(.0167) \quad (.0008) \quad (.0054) \quad (.0062)$$

Index